# FLAMMABLE

# FLAMMABLE

*Environmental Suffering
in an Argentine Shantytown*

JAVIER AUYERO

AND

DÉBORA ALEJANDRA SWISTUN

OXFORD
UNIVERSITY PRESS
2009

# OXFORD

UNIVERSITY PRESS

Oxford University Press, Inc., publishes works that further
Oxford University's objective of excellence
in research, scholarship, and education.

Oxford  New York
Auckland  Cape Town  Dar es Salaam  Hong Kong  Karachi
Kuala Lumpur  Madrid  Melbourne  Mexico City  Nairobi
New Delhi  Shanghai  Taipei  Toronto

With offices in
Argentina  Austria  Brazil  Chile  Czech Republic  France  Greece
Guatemala  Hungary  Italy  Japan  Poland  Portugal  Singapore
South Korea  Switzerland  Thailand  Turkey  Ukraine  Vietnam

Published by Oxford University Press, Inc.
198 Madison Avenue, New York, New York 10016

www.oup.com

Oxford is a registered trademark of Oxford University Press

Library of Congress Cataloging-in-Publication Data
Auyero, Javier.
Flammable : environmental suffering in an Argentine
shantytown / Javier Auyero and Débora Alejandra Swistun.
p.  cm.
Includes bibliographical references and index.
ISBN 978-0-19-537294-6; 978-0-19-537293-9 (pbk.)
1. Slums—Argentina—Buenos Aires Metropolitan Area.
2. Poor—Argentina—Buenos Aires.
3. Hazardous wastes—Argentina—Buenos Aires Metropolitan Area.
I. Swistun, Débora Alejandra.  II. Title.
HV4070.B84A99 2009
363.738′42098212—dc22    2008043342

1  3  5  7  9  8  6  4  2

Printed in the United States of America
on acid-free paper

*To the memory of Chuck Tilly*
*and his invisible elbow*

Que los que esperan no cuenten las horas,
Que los que matan se mueran del miedo.
—Joaquín Sabina, "Noche de Bodas"

———————————————

[T]he deeper the theoretical analysis goes, the closer
it gets to the data of observation.
—Pierre Bourdieu, *The Bachelors' Ball*

# Contents

# FLAMMABLE

# Introduction

## Sandra's Suffering

In 1987 Sandra Martinez[1] moved to Flammable shantytown (Villa Inflamable, located in Dock Sud, Buenos Aires). She was seven years old. At the time, her parents were working in the then federally owned YPF (Yacimientos Petrolíferos Fiscales) oil refinery. After a few years of long commutes from Florencio Varela, Sandra's parents found a place to live right across the compound that houses YPF (now Repsol), Shell, and other petrochemical companies and storage facilities. They have all been living in the neighborhood for the last eighteen years.

Sandra is now twenty-five, is married to Carlos Martinez, and has four children. Both Carlos and Sandra used to work as cleaners in two of the companies of the compound, but they lost their jobs years ago. These days, Carlos leaves the house every afternoon to scavenge around the center of Avellaneda, "up and down Avenida Mitre." "On a good week, I make around $25 (US $8). Sometimes I bring stuff to sell, a pair of sneakers or something I find in the street. And I make 5 or 10 pesos. It all depends on the kind of merchandise I bring, but now the streets are empty. It's tough. But some people give me cardboards or newspapers, some other people give me clothes or sneakers, and I sell that stuff. And we subsist...with her *plan*, we have nothing else." Sandra has not been able to find a job and is currently a beneficiary of the Plan Jefas y Jefes, an unemployment subsidy of $150 per month (US $50) that the federal government launched after the 2001 economic collapse in Argentina. "Together," she says, "we make around $250 (US $82 per month)...and with that we make ends meet (*con eso tiramos*). We cook once a day, at night." For lunch, their children have bread and milk; their only full meal is dinner. On the weekends, the family attends communal soup kitchens: "On Saturdays and Sundays we always go there, so that they can eat at least once," Sandra tells us. Their gas carafe costs $24; "we don't always have the money to pay for it, and we have to use wood [for cooking and heating]." Carlos tried to sign up for the

Plan Jefas y Jefes "but nothing happened. I did all the paperwork, and nothing came through."

The Martinezes' pressing economic needs compete for their attention with the constant health problems of two of their children. "Two of them," Sandra remarks, "have problems. The other two came out well." The youngest one, Julian, is now five, and has had convulsions since he was a baby:

> He was born with a mark in his head. The doctors told me it was nothing. That it was just a birth mark. He then started to have convulsions and I began to go from one hospital to another. At the Children's Hospital, he had a tomography done, and it turns out that his brain is affected by that mark, which is not just on the outside but inside too. And now he has that angioma that is popping out. See, Julian, show it to them.

When Julian shows us the protruding red pimple, we ask Sandra about the doctors' diagnosis. "They don't explain anything to me," she replies. "They don't know why he has that mark. I had my testing done, his father was also tested. And we have nothing. They didn't screen us for lead because they have to charge us for that. And we couldn't pay." Julian was prescribed an anticonvulsant. Sandra receives a bottle of Epamil a month for free at the local public hospital, "but Julian uses two or three bottles. And it's $18 to $20 each one, and sometimes we can't afford it. I began the paperwork to see if I can get it for free. Everybody promised me but nothing happened. Papers, papers, papers . . . nothing but words." Julian needs to be routinely supervised for his convulsions, but it has been a while since his last checkup.

> We now have an appointment for August. He could die before then, but *I have to wait* [our emphasis]. Sometimes he has convulsions twice a day, and I have no medication. Now I don't even have money to [pay for the bus to] go to the hospital. Children here are always sick, with bronchitis, with a cold. She [referring to Sofia, her seven-year-old daughter] always has headaches and stomachaches.

Sofia was born with her left leg significantly shorter than her right one. When Sandra had her first ultrasound, she was told that Sofia "was going to come out with problems. When I told the doctors that I was living here, they told me I should have my lead level tested. I couldn't afford the exams. The doctors told me that the lead may have caused the problem of the leg." Lately, Sofia began to show signs of serious learning difficulties at school: "She has problems remembering the numbers . . . it's really hard for her."

Sandra herself is not in better shape. She looks much older than twenty-five. Half of her teeth are missing, and she always looks extremely tired: "I have all the symptoms," she says referring to possible lead poisoning, "I had cramps, blood coming out of my nose, constant headaches. It's been three or four years now since I've been aching all over." When the pain is unbearable, she attends the local health center, "and the doctors give me some aspirin. I get better but then the pain comes back. At night is even worse." When we asked about her lead levels, she tells us that the tests are very expensive for her to afford: "They are between $100 and $200" (US $33 and US $67).

Sandra knows that she is not the only one with an aching body and with sick children. The problem, she says, "is all over."

> I don't really understand numbers, but my nephew has 50 percent of lead [referring to $50\,\mu g/dl$ (micrograms per deciliter); anything above $10\,\mu g/dl$ is considered poisonous]. My sister was able to pay for the lead tests because her husband works at Shell. She knew she had high levels of lead when she was pregnant.... But she is not doing anything about it. She is not in any treatment because she might cause trouble to her husband, who works at Shell. If they find out that she has been tested, he might lose his job. Sometimes I want to kill her. It is as if they are scared. But I believe the children come first. What about her children's lives? Her kid is not gaining any weight. He is very thin, and he looks yellowish. He has tons of problems, but she doesn't do anything about them. There are many, many kids with problems here.

Asked about the local doctors' reactions to these troubles, she reacts: "Nothing, they say nothing. One of the doctors left because she began to feel sick, and she found out she had lead in her blood. She'd been here only a year, so imagine how we are." During the course of our conversation, Sandra says that although she wants to leave Flammable, she has not looked seriously into how to do it. She suspects that the decision may soon be made for her, however. Like many of her neighbors in shantytown, Sandra thinks that a census that municipal staff are carrying out in the neighborhood is related to a possible relocation: "A million times they promise things. They said they were going to move us out, that they were going to make new houses for us, but there're just promises. Nobody believes anything anymore. People are really burnt out here. Shell wants this piece of land. And here, in this area of the neighborhood, we are only twenty-two families, so it is quite easy to remove us from here.... I do want to leave. Sometimes you can't be outside, the odor stinks, your throat stings. It smells of gas. Even if we close our doors, it smells."

## What This Book Is About

Like the other five thousand or so inhabitants of this fence-line community, the Martinezes are playthings of environmental, economic, and political misfortunes that are not of their own making. The Martinezes' troubled lives illustrate the devastating effects of toxic contamination on the young bodies and minds of Flammable residents. Theirs is also a story, common to other territories of urban relegation in Argentina, of dire need in an economy from which work has been disappearing and in a country whose government has almost completely abandoned them. Many Flammable residents live each day with fears about the origins and prognosis of their (and their loved ones') infirmities, uncertainties regarding relocation efforts (un)coordinated by the local government, confusions stemming from physicians' confusing interventions, and suspicions and rumors concerning the actions of the most powerful company of the compound, Shell. The product of a two-and-one-half-year-long collaborative ethnography, this book describes the life-threatening effects of environmental contamination in Flammable and explains the (sometimes puzzling and contradictory) meanings its residents ascribe to it. The large question this study addresses is the following: How do people make sense of (and cope with) toxic danger? The Martinezes' story anticipates the complexity of the answer(s): physical and psychological suffering is compounded by doubts, disagreements, suspicions, fears, and endless waiting.

Flammable is surrounded by one of the largest petrochemical compounds in the country, by a highly polluted river that flows with the toxic waste of tanneries and other industries, by a hazardous waste incinerator, and by an unmonitored landfill. As a result, Flammable's soil, air, and water streams are highly polluted with lead, chromium, benzene, and other chemicals—as are the people who live on that soil, breathe that air, and drink that water. In this book, we document this ongoing slow-motion human and environmental disaster, focusing most of our attention on the ways in which it is experienced by Flammable residents. Contrary to what most of the literature on environmental movements taught us to expect in cases such as this (i.e., emergence of a shared oppositional consciousness about the sources and effects of pollution, followed by protracted and sometimes successful collective action), Flammable is a story of a people's confusion, mistakes, and/or blindness regarding the toxicity that surrounds them. Flammable is also a story of silent habituation to contamination and of almost complete absence of mass protest against toxic onslaught.

This book seeks answers to the following (admittedly broad) questions: What are the modes of experiencing environmental suffering? How do neighbors make sense of their risky surroundings? Do residents who have for years been exposed to a poisoned environment get used to noxious fumes, polluted waters, and contaminated grounds? Since they have been regularly exposed, are they attuned to the regularities of a dirty and contaminated place? How much do they know about their toxic habitat? When (and why) do they fail to understand what is objectively a clear and present danger? And what is the relationship between this knowledge, their suffering, and their apparent collective inaction?

Knowledge about a poisoned environment, Flammable teaches us, is not solely shaped by what we see and smell and touch. Smells from chemicals, the stench from highly visible open-air dumping sites, and odors coming from lowlands filled with putrid waters through which many neighbors traverse daily are not the only influence on the residents' understanding of the environment. Experience of that polluted reality is, this book shows, *socially and politically produced*; the meanings of contamination are the outcome of power relations between residents and outside actors. These produced meanings, in turn, shape those very same unequal relationships. If the reader pays close attention to Sandra's story, she will realize that the Martinezes and their neighbors are not just being exposed to the toxins. In the opening story we see that doctors and government officials are as much a part of the everyday life of Flammable as lead and noxious odors are. So are Shell and other compound personnel. Schoolteachers, journalists, and lawyers are also part and parcel of daily life in Flammable. Together, all these actors contribute to what Flammable residents know about their place. They also influence what they ignore, what they want to know, and what they misrecognize. Government officials, company personnel, physicians, teachers, journalists, and lawyers jointly (but hardly cooperatively, given that their opinions don't count equally) shape locals' experiences of contamination and risk. This book examines how and why this production of shared knowledge (or lack thereof) occurs.

Flammable residents are alternately angry and confused or mystified about the source, extent, and potential effects of contamination. Divisions between old-timers and newcomers flourish, and rumors run rampant regarding the imminent relocation of the neighborhood and bribes paid by Shell and other companies to calm down a never-realized protest. Adding to residents' frustration is government inaction on needs ranging from the unemployment subsidy that never materialized and the much-needed medicine that failed to come through to the lead screening that was not covered by the state and thus was never carried out. As much as disappointment suffuses the lives of Flammable residents, so do dreamlike hopes: many a neighbor is expecting a hefty compensation that lawyers are believed to be on the brink of obtaining from the companies for their present toxic damage. All in all, confusions, bewilderments, divisions, rumors, frustrations, and hopes are making Flammable residents *wait*—they wait for more testing, for further and better knowledge, for relocation, and for the "huge" settlement with one of the "powerful companies" that will, in the words of a neighbor, "allow us to move out." This waiting is, as we will show, one of the ways in which Flammable residents experience submission. In a general sense, then, this book is about environmental suffering and its intricate, complex ties with social domination. In particular, this book seeks to unravel the black box of "symbolic violence." This term was coined by Pierre Bourdieu to uncover the ways in which domination works: it does so via the misrecognition of power structures on the part of the dominated. This term is usually invoked in studies of durable inequalities but is rarely examined in its concrete empirical manifestations. By dissecting the actors and processes involved in the operation of symbolic violence, we will unravel the mystery of why poor people sometimes accept deadly subordination. In other words, how is domination exercised with the subaltern's complicity? (Bourdieu 1991; Bourdieu and Wacquant 1992). This subordination, we will show, appears logical in the context of what we call "toxic uncertainty"—a way of experiencing toxic suffering that is shaped by what we call, borrowing from Charles Tilly (1996), the interacting "invisible elbows" of external power forces and of everyday routine survival struggles.[2]

## Toxic Experiences

We are certainly not the first to study the ways in which people think and feel about toxic dangers. Public understandings of health-threatening environmental contamination have been the object of many detailed research reports. A number of studies have chronicled the origins, development, and outcomes of collective actions organized against the presence of pollutants in several communities in the United States and have simultaneously examined the views and sentiments of affected residents (Levine 1982; Brown and Mikkelsen 1990; Bullard 1990; Couch and Kroll-Smith 1991; Checker 2005; Lerner 2005).[3] Although diverging in methodology, analytic depth, and empirical focus, a typical sequence can be extracted from most of these accounts:

collective ignorance about the presence and effects of toxins is interrupted when a neighbor or a group of them, in many cases "irate housewives turned into activists" (Mazur 1991:200), begins to make the connections between their place of residence and the existence of certain illnesses, between illness and toxic hazards, and between his or her individual problems and those of others. Brown and Mikkelsen (1990) coined the term "popular epidemiology" to refer to the process through which victims detect a disease pattern; the case these authors closely reconstruct is a leukemia cluster in Woburn, Massachusetts. This process of discovery of danger, of increasing awareness about the effects of surrounding toxins, is usually spearheaded by residents-turned-activists: Larry Wilson in Yellow Creek, Key Jones and Kathleen Varady in Pennsylvania, Anne Anderson in Woburn, Margie Richard in Diamond, and the now legendary Lois Gibbs in Love Canal are the best-known examples of stubborn, almost heroic, leaders of "long and bitter" (Clarke 1991) struggles. The typical sequence also includes an active process of learning and a great deal of frustration, in which victims become skilled at playing political games with authorities and quickly absorbing scientific knowledge.

Despite divergent theoretical orientations, most of the available accounts seem to share a classical Marxist model of consciousness: physically proximate aggrieved people overcome false beliefs or persistent uncertainties through reflection and interaction. The outcome of the "loss of innocence" (Levine 1982; Cable and Walsh 1991) is almost always a single and determined consensus regarding the problem and its solution—tellingly, the main actor in most of the chronicles is "the community." In emphasizing changes in collective perceptions of legitimacy and mutability of objective conditions, most works portray—either implicitly or explicitly—a variation of what Doug McAdam termed, a while ago, "cognitive liberation," which he defined as the "transformation from hopeless submission to oppressive conditions to an aroused readiness to challenge those conditions" (1982:34). Most of these studies, furthermore, examine risk perceptions as *independent variables*: beliefs about hazards are used to explain behavioral outcomes (i.e., the collective actions that people organize to protect themselves; see Tierney 1999). The *sources* of such perceptions usually remain underexplored (for an exception, see Beamish 2001; see also Heimer 1988).

The extant literature leaves cases such as Flammable in the shadows because it focuses almost exclusively on cases in which communities were either relocated, compensated, and/or cleaned, and it emphasizes the ultimate achievement of a shared consensus regarding sources, effects, and solutions to contamination—communities that "discover" and become knowledgeable about their toxicity. Most of what we know about environmental injustice and the emergence of collective action against those responsible for contamination is of little analytic help to understand and explain cases in which there is neither a clear outcome nor a consensus on the very existence of a problem, much less a potential solution. When confronted not with cognitive liberation and protest but with the reproduction of ignorance, doubts, disagreements, and fears, we are at an analytical and theoretical loss.

As we said above, many people in Flammable know about contamination but interpret the information in different and sometimes contradictory ways. Others ignore or are uncertain about the presence of toxins in the environment and about the relationship between exposure and disease. Many others lack the means of assessing causes or assigning blame. When confronted with cases such as Flammable in which residents are divided and confused, a place where ignorance and doubts about toxicity are routinely reproduced and risk is constantly normalized, we thus need to resort to an alternative framework, one that makes the perpetuation of ignorance, mistake, and confusion the center of analysis. In Flammable, what needs to be explained is not the achievement of a collective "we" and the simultaneous genesis of collective action but the reproduction of uncertainty, misunderstanding, division, and, ultimately, inaction in the midst of sustained toxic assault. The "not-knowing" and the "doubting" claim for an explanation; they are constitutive parts of the way in which social domination works and of the residents' toxic suffering.

Let us reiterate our broad questions: How do people who are routinely exposed to toxic hazards, whose lives are in constant danger, think and feel about their surroundings? What set of practices accompany these feelings and cognitions?

Scholarship on risk perception has significantly expanded during the last two decades (Dietz et al. 1989; Stallings 1990; Clarke and Short 1993; Tierney 1999; Caplan 2000) emphasizing the socially constructed character of the varying ways in which lay persons (Heimer 1988; Beamish 2001), policy-makers (Jasanoff 1986), organizations (Clarke 1989; Vaughan 1990, 2004; Eden 2004), and communities (Erickson 1976; Edelstein 2003) understand risk and assess hazards.

Schemata of perception (Bourdieu 1977, 1998, 2000), cognitive structures (DiMaggio 1997), or organizational frames (Vaughan 1998, 2004; Eden 2004) mediate between the hazardous environment and the subjective experiences of it and give form to what people know, think they know, ignore, or interpret about surrounding dangers. A plethora of social influences shape these frames or schemata. Existing sociological research recognizes the roles of organizations (Stallings 1990; Clarke and Short 1993; Perrow 1997), institutional interests (Clarke 1989, 1990; Tierney 1999), expert systems (Proctor 1995; Beamish 2001), and the state (Freudenburg 1993; Pollak 1996) in the molding of lay-public "risk frames." The trust, or lack thereof, that people have in organizations and expert systems in charge of producing information about risk, those responsible for protecting the public, and the producers of hazards are directly relevant for risk perceptions (Freudenburg 1993; Perrow 1997; Beamish 2001). To understand and explain the widespread uncertainty and confusion that dominate the lives of people living at risk, empirical research needs not only to delve deep into the frames actors use to perceive their surroundings but also to find out why these frames are as they are (Heimer 1988; Tierney 1999). As Beamish (2001:11) argues, "historical legacy" and "interpretive context" are central in giving form to perceptions of risk.

Cognitive psychologists have also contributed to our understanding and explanation of the ways in which individuals perceive risk. Through a variety of ingenious laboratory experiments, they documented a series of heuristics on which individuals rely to simplify the selection and digestion of an overabundance of information under conditions of uncertainty (Kahneman, Slovic, and Tversky 1982; Gilovich, Griffin, and Kahneman 2002). Two of these cognitive heuristics are of particular relevance to our study of risk perceptions: "availability" and "anchoring." "Availability" refers to the tendency individuals have to give excessive importance to information that, for reasons that are logically accidental, grabs their attention. "Anchoring" induces people to give undue weight to an initial value which in turn powerfully affects their subsequent judgments. In other words, people's estimations of risk are affected by the availability of information and by the reference point that frames their cognitive mapping of the situation. Heimer (1988) rightly notes that sociological studies of risk perception should contextualize these inferential shortcuts by specifying the factors that influence the availability of information and where the reference points come from.[4] In this book, we will do so by dissecting the ways in which diverse powerful actors' striking but contradictory claims about existing hazards shape the availability of information about the origins and effects of toxic contamination and by examining the anchoring of perceptions in the history of a neighborhood and its daily routines and interactions.

Most of the research conducted on "contaminated communities" (Edelstein 2003) focuses on cases in which everyday life is abruptly dislocated by the uncovering of nearby hazards. The "disruption of the quotidian" (Snow et al.

1998) begins with initial suspicions regarding the existence of dangerous toxins in the vicinity of a residential area and their potential or actual effects on residents' health. As we stated above, these initial qualms are typically followed by a process of discovery through popular epidemiology and are accompanied by a consensus regarding sources of and solutions to the problem—that is, an emerging new frame (Levine 1982; Brown and Mikkelsen 1990; Brown 1991; Capek 1993; Murphree et al. 1996; Clapp 2002). Risk frames, in the typical sequence uncovered by existing scholarship, emerge in interaction with other aggrieved parties (some of whom quickly surface as leaders) and in confrontation with the government and other expert systems, physicians being prominent among them, which typically deny, cover up, or minimize the actual or potential damage (Levine 1982; Clarke 1989; Brown and Mikkelsen 1990; Bryson et al. 2001; Phillimore et al. 2000; Beamish 2000, 2002; Petryna 2002; Gephart 2004; Lerner 2005).

Collective perceptions of risk have rarely been scrutinized in specific sociospatial universes, such as Flammable, in which daily life is dominated by ignorance, errors, and doubts regarding sources and effects of toxicity and in which the minimization or denial by socially consequential actors is not a straightforward process.[5] In our analysis we heed the call for a radical contextualization of the heuristic devices and frames that actors draw upon to make sense of hazards (Heimer 1988; Vaughan 1990, 1998, 1999, 2004; Eden 2004) in order to explain the sociopolitical production of toxic uncertainty. To foreshadow our argument: during the seventy-year period in which health-threatening pollution incubated in the neighborhood, neither a major industrial accident nor a sudden discovery of a disease cluster ever disrupted daily routines. This temporal dispersion of contamination resulted in what we label, combining insights from cognitive psychology and organizational sociology, the *relational anchoring of risk perceptions* (Eden 2004; Vaughan 2004; Kahneman, Slovic, and Tversky 1982; Gilovich, Griffin, and Kahneman 2002). We argue that uninterrupted routines and interactions work smoothly as blinders to increasing environmental hazards. During the long period of slowly germinating contamination, the actions of government authorities toward pollution in the neighborhood were less consistent and more contradictory than either the denial or underestimation that has been documented in the existing literature. Those multiple incongruous actions gave shape to what we term, extending the insights of students of ideology and symbolic power (Thompson 1984; Eagleton 1991; Bourdieu 1991), a *labor of confusion* that has a decisive effect on shared (mis)understandings.

The work of social scientists who have studied the aftermath of disasters (Erickson 1976; Das 1995; Petryna 2002) will also guide our exploration of the form and origins of Flammable's toxic experience. This body of scholarship agrees that, far from being shaped exclusively by the physical world, knowledge about the environment is "a veritable social institution whose origin sociology alone can retrace and explain" (Durkheim and Mauss 1963:3). To take one classic example: In his work on the individual and collective traumas created by the Buffalo Creek flood, Kai Erikson (1976) examines the effects of the disappearance of the relational support that allows people to "camouflage" the constant presence of danger. When a community is destroyed, Erikson asserts, people cannot be part of the "conspiracy to make a perilous world seem safe" (240); they become unable to "edit reality in such a way that it seems manageable" (240). This masking of hazards, Erikson's work clearly shows, is collective, relational work.

The classic and current scholarship of which we here take heed does not deny the existence of an objective (in our case, polluted) reality outside the social. It highlights, however, that the knowledge of this reality is

> always, and profoundly, mediated by the social: what actors already know, what they want to know, how they think they can go about learning more, and the criteria by which they judge and make new knowledge—all these are not found in nature but are socially determined. (Eden 2004:50)

Between the (contaminated) environment and the subjective experiences of it we find cognitive frames that, deeply influenced by history and by discursive and practical interventions, shape toxic knowledge (or lack thereof). To understand and explain Flammable's toxic confusion we therefore need to delve deep into these schemata through which residents think and feel about their surroundings and find out why these frames are how they are.[6] This insight will take center stage when confronted with the errors, blindness, and mystifications (the "toxic confusion") that being quite common among Flammable residents constitute the main subject of our book.

Flammable has been (and still is at the time of this writing) in the news. If the reader takes a look at the many reports on the area where the neighborhood is located published by Argentine national newspapers or aired on national television she would be inclined to think that people there know all about the contamination. Two and a half years of observation and conversations made us realize that the picture people present to themselves is less sharply drawn than the one they sketch for outsiders. We here focus on the origins, forms, and effects of those nuances as they appear in the flow of daily life. We are here particularly interested in how people in Flammable don't know or doubt what they know or are confused about what they think they know.

True, toxic contamination is "inherently uncertain" (Edelstein 2003): the body's past exposures, the dose-response relationship, synergistic effects, and etiological ambiguity all contribute to the problem of haziness in both toxicology and epidemiology (Brown, Kroll-Smith, and Gunter 2000).[7] In Flammable, this intrinsic uncertainty is amplified by the practical and discursive interventions of compound personnel, doctors, government officials, and lawyers. This book seeks to unravel the social logic and the outcomes of the poisonous puzzlements that, together with sheer toxic assault, afflict Flammable residents.

Contemporary urban ethnography in the Americas has done a splendid job in describing and explaining the causes and experiential forms of the sufferings endured by dwellers in ghettos, inner cities, *favelas, villas, comunas,* and other territories of urban relegation. Even in the midst of their distress caused by everyday, structural, symbolic, or political violence (Bourgois 2001), most of the protagonists of urban ethnography remain coherent subjects—actors who are angry or happy, scared or courageous, and who, most relevant for the case at hand, usually know something that we do not. We rarely see ethnographic texts in which people hesitate, make mistakes, and/or are plagued by contradictions—subjects who are angry and happy, scared and courageous, subjects who know and don't know. Uncertainty and ignorance have not been a dominant focus among ethnographers; understandably so because, as Murray Last (1992:393) writes, "it is hard enough to record what they do know" (for exceptions, see Clarke 1989; Das 1995; and Vaughan 1990, 1998). Our book will zoom in on the complex, sometimes incongruous or perplexing ways in which Flammable residents make sense of their toxic surroundings. Besides the case of environmental suffering and its relationship with social domination in the particular sociosymbolic universe of Flammable, this book seeks to contribute to a general understanding and explanation of the social production of confusion—its reasons and effects.

## Cubist Ethnography

As it will become clear, Flammable is routinely visited by outsiders, including media reporters, lawyers, doctors, and activists. Early on in the fieldwork, the nonresident Javier realized that neighbors have a ready-made discourse for these visitors. This narrative repertoire consistently tells outsiders: "It's all contaminated here, everybody is sick." Flammable is known to the outside as a polluted, dreadful place—one national newspaper published a story about the neighborhood titled "The Inferno Exists, and It Is Located in Dock Sud." Neighbors rightly assume that outsiders come to them to talk about contamination and about how awful life is across from the petrochemical compound.

The presentation of the contaminated and damaged self that outsiders are faced with and are deceived by has a backstage, and things look and sound quite different there. We were able to access this backstage not by some suspect chameleonic transformation but by conducting team ethnographic research, and herein lies the methodological innovation of this work. Javier Auyero conducted most of the interviews with officials, company personnel, activists, and lawyers and did the necessary archival work. Débora Swistun conducted most of the interviews with residents and recorded their life stories. She has lived most of her life in the neighborhood; most of the people she talked to for this project are her neighbors. Some of them have known her since she was born, and many are friends or acquaintances of her family.[8]

After we agreed on the basic premises of our research, we discussed different interview topics and participant observation strategies. The interviews were carried out more as conversations among neighbors than as the typical exchange of information that, despite best intentions and good rapport, still dominates this particular kind of social relationship. Familiarity and social proximity helped to reduce the symbolic violence exerted through the interview relationship (Bourdieu et al. 1999) and to circumvent the narrative repertoire available for outsiders. By avoiding the outsiders' intrusion and its activation of the repertoire that deceives the researcher—by reducing distance and minimizing asymmetry—we were able to have research experiences similar to those that Bourdieu and his collaborators assert they had when conducting the interviews that led to *The Weight of the World*. We also had a feeling of being privy to an "induced and accompanied self analysis" (Bourdieu et al. 1999). Many a resident took advantage of the opportunity afforded by the interview to conduct a more or less gratifying, more or less painful, self-examination.

Division of practical labor aside, we carried out this project together since the very beginning and we were, jointly, confronted with complicated issues. To begin with, we had to educate ourselves in environmental and biomedical research. In the process, we discovered that uncertainties are not only widespread among Flammable residents but also among scientists, physicians, epidemiologists, engineers, and other experts (see, for example, Proctor 1995;

Brown and Mikkelsen 1990; Brown et al. 2000; D. Davis 2002; Phillimore et al. 2000). Most of the technical details, regarding the air and epidemiological studies for example, are here relegated to footnotes or referred to the original sources for the sake of the text's simplicity.

Our research involved us in various distressing moments, as when, during interviews or informal conversations, extremely worried mothers called their sons or daughters to show us their disfigurements or injuries—"Gonzalo, show them your hand," "Mami, show them your head," "See, touch me here [pointing at his head], it's all bumpy"—and/or voiced doubts regarding the possible effects of pollution in their loved ones' precarious health. Along the way, and as a result of our collaborative fieldwork, Débora realized that her own health problems were likely consequences of lifetime residence in Flammable. Toward the end of the book, we closely examine this self-transformative process.

Flammable is a neglected place, the plight of its inhabitants ignored or misrepresented; the last thing we wanted to do in the personal interactions on which our research is based was to reproduce this public disregard. We did our best to learn how to listen, look, and touch with respect and care, knowing with Nancy Scheper-Hughes (1992:28) that "seeing, listening, touching, recording, can be, if done with care and sensitivity, acts of fraternity and sisterhood, acts of solidarity. Above all, they are the work of recognition. Not to look, not to touch, not to record, can be the hostile act, the act of indifference and of turning away." We also did our best to avoid being perceived as occasional visitors who routinely come to the neighborhood and then all too soon disappear without a trace. The book might have taken longer to complete than the people who opened their homes to us expected, but we hope it will be seen as proof that their time and their sometime painful testimonies were not lost.

Together with interviews and life stories, we relied on photography to get a better sense of residents' views and experiences of their surroundings. Relying upon some of the insights of visual sociology (Becker 1995; Wagner 2001; Harper 2003), we asked students at the local school to take pictures of their neighborhood (of the aspects they like and those they dislike), and we discussed the photographs with them.

We use youngsters' images and voices as a window into their lived experience of contamination. A number of phrases were repeated over and over again in students' descriptions of the photos: "See all this garbage that sits in front of my house"; "This [dirty swamp] is my uncle's backyard," "Look at this...it's all mud...it's all contaminated...this is where we play." These photos and voices are here appreciated as youngsters' representations of the ways in which they perceive their relationships with the environment and with the adjacent petrochemical compound. We draw upon these representations to introduce the reader into Flammable.

The analysis that follows is based on images, interviews, life stories, and, most importantly, direct observation. In other words, the text is to a great extent based on traditional ethnographic fieldwork here understood as "social research based on the close-up, on-the-ground observation of people and institutions in real time and space, in which the investigator embeds herself near (or within) the phenomenon so as to detect how and why agents on the scene act, think and feel the way they do" (Wacquant 2003:5; see also Wacquant 1995). Applying the evidentiary criteria that is normally used for ethnographic research (Becker 1958; Katz 1982), we assign higher evidentiary value to conduct we were able to observe versus behavior reported by interviewees to have occurred, individual acts or patterns of conduct recounted by many observers versus those recounted by only one. As much as we focused attention in readily observable phenomena, we soon discovered that rumors about things that have occurred or that they are about to take place are part and parcel of Flammable's reality. This is a place riddled not only with toxics but also by sometimes verifiable stories regarding the past and future actions of the local government, of the compound's companies, and of lawyers and media reporters. When we were able to corroborate the veracity of these rumors, we note that in the text. Some stories could not be authenticated—for example, those regarding bribes a company supposedly pays to prevent journalists from publishing damaging news or to keep neighbors from protesting. We did, however, pay analytic attention to these stories because they are an essential part of living in this dangerous place knowing full well that, in the analysis of the experience of pollution, it is not a matter of what this or that company or this or that government official really are or do but how they are perceived to be and to behave.

Many of the people in Flammable believe that Shell's activities there, such as building the local health center or providing funds for the local school, are done with wicked intentions: Shell does what it does in the community to "cover up." "They cure us because they contaminate us," we repeatedly heard. Many others are persuaded that government officials allow this to happen because "they are all corrupt" and "there's a lot of money involved." The task of this book is not to engage in a trial regarding the companies—Shell, Repsol, Petrobras, and others—and the state. Occasionally, however, we give due attention to these attributions of intentions because, again, they are part and parcel of the way residents think and feel about their polluted place, and they are a crucial element of the residents' suffering. As will become clear, Flammable residents are frustrated with and confused by government actions and inaction, are puzzled by the seemingly contradictory behavior of doctors and oil company personnel, are simultaneously hopeful and angry with the reporters who "use" them, and are trusting and suspicious of lawyers. In what follows, objective contamination and its subjective experience are brought together for a better understanding of what living in harm's way is all about.

Our way of apprehending and portraying the toxic experience of Flammable residents takes heed of Cubism's main lesson: the essence of an object is captured only by showing it simultaneously from multiple points of view. This principle is especially important when the object is as elusive as toxic experience. Our research draws on the different fieldwork strategies and diverse theoretical traditions; our evidence is presented through a combination of different narrative and analytic styles. The authors not only live in different places but also come from different disciplines. (Javier lives in Austin, Texas, and is a sociologist; Débora, an anthropologist, lived until June 2007 in Villa Inflamable, Buenos Aires.) We both, however, believe in the virtues and potentials of interdisciplinary collaboration, particularly for the study of social suffering.[9]

## On Environmental Suffering

Social suffering has recently received long-deserved attention in the social sciences, particularly in anthropology and sociology. The causes and experiences of suffering have been scrutinized from a variety of theoretical perspectives and in a wide array of empirical universes (Kleinman 1988; Kleinman, Das, and Lock 1997; Das 1995; Klinenberg 2002; Todeschini 2001; Bourdieu 1999; Sayad 2004; Ashforth 2005; for a summary of existing literature, see Wilkinson 2005). Suffering, most scholarship agrees, is a destructive experience, something that is "against us" (Wilkinson 2005). Our focus here is not on suffering as an individual experience (Scarry 1987) but on the experiences of affliction that are "actively created and distributed by the social order itself" (Das 1995; see also Klinenberg 2002), suffering as the product of agents' position in the social space—or what Bourdieu would call a social "site effect." Although deep, systematic accounts of the lived experiences of suffering do not abound (Wilkinson 2005), medical anthropology and some ethnographic work in sociology have recently provided vivid examinations of what suffering does to people and of how they make sense of it (Bourgois 2003; Bourgois and Schonberg forthcoming; Scheper-Hughes 1994; Farmer 2003). This process of "making sense of" suffering is never an individual product. Although suffering is indeed located in individual bodies, these "bear the stamp of the authority of society upon the docile bodies of its members" (Das 1995:138). Sufferers do not experience their predicament as isolated Robinson Crusoes but in power-laden relational settings. These contexts give form to the ways in which affliction is lived and understood.

Our book focuses its attention on environmental suffering—a particular form of social suffering caused by the concrete polluting actions of specific actors—and on the factors that mold the experience of this suffering. Flammable residents' suffering is sometimes appropriated, other times denied or amplified, by existing institutions, usually for the sake of their own legitimation (Das 1995). We will closely examine the ways in which residents make sense of their suffering in constant dialogue with these institutions. We will also document the gender of this affliction: As the reader will soon notice when reading the many stories presented in the following chapters, the burden of the environmental suffering documented here falls largely on the mothers of Flammable. Given their disproportionate share of the work involved in child care, they are the ones who constantly worry about and attend to their children's health. Mothers bear the brunt of responsibility for care and, sometimes, the brunt of the blame: lead contamination is frequently seen in the neighborhood as evidence of "bad mothers." Given the work schedules of their male partners, women are the ones who typically call lawyers to make appointments and who travel to government offices to demand aid. Women also follow the news about possible relocation and compensation more closely. In order to better understand the relationship between toxic experiences and social domination, we should thus pay closer attention to this important gender dimension and to the ways it interacts and reinforces the class aspects of environmental suffering.

Environmental suffering is hardly a top scholarly concern these days. Although existing literature on urban environmental problems in Latin America certainly raises the issue (Lemos 1998; Pezzoli 2000; Evans 2002; Hochstetler and Keck 2007), the miserable physical environment where the urban poor live remain a marginal preoccupation among students of poverty in Latin America. To witness: a recent comprehensive review of studies of poverty and inequality in Latin America (Hoffman and Centeno 2003) and a symposium on the history and state of the studies of marginality and exclusion in Latin America published in the most prominent journal of Latin American studies (González de la Rocha et al. 2004) make no mention of environmental factors as key determinants in the reproduction of destitution and inequity.[10]

With a few notable exceptions (Scheper-Hughes 1994; Paley 2001; Farmer 2004) ethnographies of urban poverty and marginality in Latin America have also failed to take into account the simple fact that the poor do not breathe the same air, drink the same water, or play on the same soil as the nonpoor do. Poor people's lives do not unfold on the head of a pin; theirs is an often polluted environment that has dire consequences for their present health and their future capabilities. That environmental factors are key determinants in the reproduction of destitution and inequity is a matter about which scholars (us included) have remained silent for too long.[11] This silence—another incarnation of what Sherry Ortner (1995) famously called "ethnographic refusal"—is shocking given how prominent a role the material context of poor people's lives plays not only in foundational texts in the study of poverty and inequality, such as Friedrich Engels's *The Conditions of the Working Class in England*, but also, and more specifically, in one of the seminal texts in the study of the lives of the urban pariahs of Latin American cities. In *Child of the Dark: The Diary of Carolina Maria de Jesus*, Carolina, a longtime resident of a favela during the 1950s, provides a firsthand account of everyday life in a shantytown located in Sao Paulo, Brazil. Carolina refers to her favela with words that will sound painfully familiar to the inhabitants of Flammable: "It is a garbage dump," she writes. "Only pigs could live in a place like this. This is the pigsty of Sao Paulo" (27). Throughout the book, she speaks of polluted waters and what she calls the "perfume" of "rotting mud (and) excrement" (40) as defining features of the lives of the poverty enclaves. Half a century later, the shantytown poor are still surrounded by filth, stench, and contaminated grounds and waters. Although our collaborative ethnography's main purpose is to examine what living in the midst of garbage and poison does to people and how they make sense of it, the book carries a larger analytical implication: research on inequality and marginality in Latin America must pay close attention to the polluted space where the urban poor live.

## What Lies Ahead

Chapter 1 provides an overview of the state and fate of shantytowns in Buenos Aires and sets their expansion into a regional and global context. Chapter 2 begins with a visual tour of Flammable that relies mainly on the photographs taken by youngsters from the local school. The chapter then relies on oral histories and archival evidence to reconstruct the history of Flammable. We also draw upon an epidemiological study conducted between 2001 and 2003 and several other reports conducted by government agencies and private researchers to describe the toxic environment of Flammable. Two dominant themes emerge in the shantytowns' history and present condition: an organic relationship with the adjacent petrochemical compound, mainly with Shell, the biggest company within it, and increasing environmental degradation.

"Toxic uncertainty" is the subject of the following two chapters. In chapter 3, we look at the ways the people who work at Shell think and feel about their neighbors. We take an in-depth look at the internal contradictions of the dominant discourse because they resonate in the ways in which Flammable residents make sense of toxic danger. Chapter 4 then presents the reader with all the "booming and buzzing" bewilderment—confusions and doubts that define local views take center stage. This chapter seeks to explain the genesis of confusion and uncertainty by dissecting the actions and discourses of other actors who intervene in Flammable. The chapter thus inspects the workings of what we term the *labor of confusion* that shapes much of the environmental suffering of Flammable residents.

Chapter 5 describes *la lucha contra el cable* (the struggle against the wire)— the only sustained collective protest organized against one company within the compound. The seven-month-long protest could not stop the installation of the high-voltage wires that neighbors claim to have harmful health effects. The protest, together with the epidemiological study, brought a stream of lawyers and potential lawsuits against some of the compound's companies to the neighborhood. Many residents now live in hope of collecting from lawsuits that will permit them to move out and buy new homes. And they are expectantly waiting: for a lawyer to come, for judges to rule, for a government official to decide on relocation. This chapter focuses attention on an aspect of the relationship between neighbors and lawyers that is crucial to understand Flammable's toxic experience: the hopes that residents place in future legal compensation for present toxic damage. The experience in Flammable of submission to domination is one of endless waiting.

In chapter 6 we analyze what we call "collective disbelief in joint action" through an examination of a series of events in which residents discuss their fate. We close this chapter with a sliver of hope for the future: when our research became public news in Argentina, Débora was offered (and accepted) a position in the federal agency in charge of environmental policy. At the time of this writing, she is working for the government on a project to improve living conditions in the neighborhood and, eventually, to relocate the residents. In the last chapter, we formalize our understanding and explanation of the social production of toxic uncertainty by pulling together all the separate threads of our analysis. We then take a reflexive turn to inspect the ways in which our joint research made an impact on Débora, the "native anthropologist," and offer further evidence and thoughts on the links between being exposed and being disposed.

In the conclusion, we come back to the literature on social suffering and we elaborate on what we think our twin ethnographic focus on toxic experience and on collective confusion adds to existing debates on the experience of affliction. The case of Flammable, we argue, should help us to inspect the complex links between material suffering and symbolic domination.

# 1

## Villas del Riachuelo
## Life amid Hazards, Garbage, and Poison

Every great city has one or more slums, where the working
class is crowded together. True, poverty often dwells in
hidden alleys close to the palaces of the rich; but, in general,
a separate territory has been assigned to it, where, removed
from the sight of the happier classes, it may struggle along as
it can....The streets are generally unpaved, rough, dirty, filled
with vegetable and animal refuse, without sewers or gutters,
but supplied with foul, stagnant pools instead.
Friedrich Engels, *The Condition of the Working Class in England*

Fifty years after their emergence in the urban landscape, shantytowns are a permanent (and expanding) part of the geography of Argentina. Despite their presence and growth, however, not much is known about these territories of urban relegation.[1] This brief chapter provides a general description of their growth in Buenos Aires and then focuses attention on one of the defining, though understudied, features of shantytowns: their unsanitary environment and its attendant health-threatening effects. Both themes will command our attention in the rest of the book.

There have been many insightful attempts to comprehend what goes on within these enclaves of *ranchos de lata*, which are situated at the very bottom of the hierarchy of urban places. Lucas Demare's early realist film *Detrás de un Largo Muro* (1957) was a first attempt to capture the lives of the *villeros*. Demare's antipopulist ideological biases should not detract his effort to portray the diversity of shantytown life—its hopes, its conflicts, its miseries. *Villa Miseria También es América*, written in 1957 by Bernardo Verbitsky, whom many credit with coining the term *villa miseria*, endeavors (to a great extent successfully) to present an intimate portrait of the lives of the urban destitute. Reading Verbitsky's book in tandem with Cristian Alarcón's recent *Cuando Me Muera Quiero Que Me Toquen Cumbia* yields a crystal-clear picture of the transition from the slums of hope to the squatter settlements of despair, to borrow an apt expression from Susan Eckstein (1990). Alarcón's vivid account of the life and death of *el frente vital* (a shanty version of a primitive rebel), of his friends and family, of the daily sufferings and limited aspirations of shantytown dwellers, offers the best available chronicle of daily life in contemporary shantytowns. His close-up portrait of the *vidas de pibes chorros* (lives of young thieves) movingly conveys the pace, the pain, and the dreams of people living in these spaces of accumulated deprivation where the hopes of upward (and outward) social mobility that characterized the 1950s shanty-dwellers portrayed by Verbitsky have almost completely vanished.

Despite these insightful and nuanced attempts, one can hardly think of an urban form that is the repository of so many misrepresentations. Shantytowns were portrayed as the ultimate example of the failure of Peronist populism during the '50s, as project sites for the modernizing dreams of the '60s, as hotbeds where revolution was thought to be germinating during the '70s, as obstacles to progress during the dictatorship of the '80s, and as places of immorality, crime, and lawlessness in contemporary Argentina. Today, hardly a conversation about public security avoids mentioning the *villa* or the *villeros* (a label that is equally applied to people living in any poor area, not just shantytowns) as a symbolic but real threat to be avoided. In today's fragmented and polarized Argentina, shantytowns are thought of as high-crime areas to be feared and avoided. When the news media report on shantytowns and their inhabitants, they overwhelmingly focus on how people from outside react to these "refuges (*aguantaderos*) of criminal activities." In a country in which urban security is a top concern, the shantytown stands out as the origin of most criminal activity, and experts on the causes and solutions of crime invariably feel the need to address the "shantytown problem." When, for example, former New York City Chief of Police William Bratton visited Buenos Aires a few years ago after being hired by a mayoral candidate as an adviser on urban security issues, he spent his first day visiting a police precinct and two of the largest shantytowns. In being tainted subjects, Argentine *villeros* are not alone. Around the world, slums and shantytowns, and their stigmatized residents, are "typically depicted from above and from afar in somber and monochrome tones" (Wacquant 2007:1; see also Neuwirth 2005).

*Villas* are Argentine versions of an increasingly global phenomenon. During the last three decades, according to a 2003 United Nations report, the presence of slums in metropolitan areas of the world has skyrocketed.[2] According to this report, roughly a third of the population of Latin America lived in slums in 2001. Drawing on this same report, social critic Mike Davis (2006:17) speaks of the last three decades as characterized by "the mass production of slums" and forecasts that

> the cities of the future, rather than being made out of glass and steel as envisioned by earlier generations of urbanists, are instead largely constructed out of crude brick, straw, recycled plastic, cement blocks, and scrap wood. Instead of cities of light soaring toward heaven, much of the twenty-first-century urban world squats in squalor, surrounded by pollution, excrement, and decay. (19)

From 2001 to 2006, the number of people living in slums, shantytowns, and squatter settlements in Greater Buenos Aires almost doubled, rising from fewer than 639,000 to more than 1.14 million. In the same time frame, the number of settlements rose from less than four hundred to a thousand.[3] According to Cravino's estimates (2007b), 10 percent of the population of the Buenos Aires metropolitan area now lives in informal settlements.[4]

Shantytown increase is a concrete manifestation of the fragmentation of Buenos Aires metropolitan space which, in turns, reflects and reinforces growing levels of social inequality (Pirez 2001; Catenazzi and Lombardo 2003). A few figures would suffice to illustrate the mounting disparity between Argentines. Together with growing unemployment and poverty, during the last three decades there has been a steady deterioration in the distribution of income in the country as a whole. As Aronskind (2001:18) summarizes: "21.5% of the population was poor in 1991, 27% at the end of 2000. Indigents were 3% of the population in 1991 and 7% in 2000. At the beginnings of the 1990s there were 1.6 million unemployed, at the end of the 2000 there are 4 million unemployed." If we take recent figures available from the National Institute of Statistics (INDEC) the rising poverty rates become quite evident. In 1986, 9.1 percent of households and 12.7 percent of people lived below the poverty line in Greater Buenos Aires. In 2002, these figures were 37.7 percent and 49.7 percent, respectively. In other words, whereas a little more than one in ten *bonaerenses* were poor twenty years ago, at the dawn of the new century one in two is living below the poverty line. Regarding inequality, one figure should suffice: the Gini coefficient went from 0.36 in 1974 to 0.51 in 2000 (Altimir et al. 2002:54).

Although the trends in poverty rates have been slowly reversing since 2003, these economic and social disparities so long in the making have become inscribed in space. Gated suburban communities (*barrios privados*, which Pirez refers to as "corridors of modernity and wealth" [2001:3]), have been booming right alongside enclaves of deprivation (Svampa 2001). These *barrios privados* and the *villas* now encapsulate the growing extremes of poverty and wealth that characterize contemporary Argentina.

But the new shantytowns are different from their urban relatives of the 1950s and 1960s. The shantytowns that spread throughout Buenos Aires and many other metropolitan areas in Latin America during the 1940s through 1960s were intimately tied to an economic model based on import substitution industrialization and its related internal mass migration (Grillo, Lacarrieu, and Raggio 1995; Yujnovsky 1984; Lomnitz 1975; Portés 1972).[5] By contrast, the explosion of shantytowns in contemporary Argentina is deeply imbricated with structural adjustment and deindustrialization. As in many other regions of the world, slum growth and industrialization are now decoupled (Rao 2006).

Although slums, shantytowns, and squatter settlements are, in Argentina and elsewhere, intimately associated with environmental risks and unsanitary living conditions, the direct health effects of specific contaminants or combinations of them in any given area are largely unknown. As Mike Davis notes, "Very little research has been conducted on environmental health [in slums], especially the risks that arise from synergies of multiple toxins and pollutants in the same location" (2006:129). Let us now introduce this neglected dimension of shanty life which will be the main subject of our analysis in the pages that follow.

Most shantytowns are built where no one wants to live. Most of the time the land's unsuitability has to do with its location vis-à-vis the larger city and access to services. In many cases, the land itself is flawed, perhaps in ways that are not obvious until a heavy rain or a mudslide or an earthquake. In the worst cases, the flaw of the location is so clear and distinct that it is obvious to all that no human being would live in such a place if not compelled by sheer desperation. In a news article about the proliferation of shantytowns in Greater Buenos Aires, the province's minister of social welfare spoke of new settlements that seemed to spring up overnight in what might seem the unlikeliest of places. "In Lomas de Zamora, we find 6 shantytowns [located] on top of garbage dumps."[6]

The authors of *The Challenge of Slums* (2003:11) put it quite clearly:

Unhealthy living conditions are the result of a lack of basic services, with visible, open sewers, lack of pathways, uncontrolled dumping of waste, polluted environments, etc. Houses may be built on hazardous locations or land unsuitable for settlement, such as floodplains, in proximity to industrial plants with toxic emissions or waste disposal sites, and on areas subject to landslip. The layout of the settlement may be hazardous because of a lack of access ways and high densities of dilapidated structures.

Mike Davis (2006:121) describes the slum ecology along similar lines, stating that a "hazardous, health-threatening location is the geographical definition of the typical squatters' settlement... [squatters are] pioneer settlers of swamps, floodplains, volcano slopes, unstable hillsides, rubbish mountains, chemical dumps, railroad sidings, and desert fringes."[7] In the technical language of UN-Habitat researchers, slums are all too often the "receivers" of a city's "negative externalities":

> Accumulations of solid waste in a city's rubbish dump represent one such negative externality. Such land has little or no economic value and, therefore, remains open to "temporary" occupancy by immigrant families with nowhere else to go. Such settlements pose enormous risks to their residents from disease, from contaminated air, water and soil, and from collapse of the dump itself. (2003:69)

This is also true for the case of Argentina. Different from most citizens living in the city of Buenos Aires and its suburbs, the *villas'* denizens do not have access to regular garbage collection. As Stillwaggon (1998:110) writes in her survey of health conditions of the country's poor, "Garbage sits in piles in the streets, a haven for disease vectors, flies, and rats.... Dogs and cats scavenge on garbage and then bring disease home." Stillwaggon also points out (74–75) that the preferred targets of infantile tuberculosis and measles are slum children (80 percent of the cases are found among children living in shantytowns). Rats and scavenging animals reappear in the story that unfolds in subsequent chapters. And so will garbage because Flammable is not only deprived of regular garbage collection but, most important, works as an open air clandestine garbage pit.

A significant proportion of the shantytown growth in Buenos Aires took place along the highly contaminated banks of the Riachuelo, the river that flows through the southern part of the metropolitan area. A recent count by the Federal Ombudsman office reports that thirteen *villas* are located on its banks. According to the Pan American Health Organization (PAHO 1990, cited in Stillwaggon 1998:110), this river receives "huge amounts of heavy metals and organic compounds owing to the discharge of industrial waste." Tons of toxic sludge, diluted solvents (dumped by meat-packing plants, chemical industries, tanneries, and households), as well as lead and cadmium are routinely tossed into the Riachuelo's dead stream.[8] It is no coincidence that the Riachuelo has been defined by the Federal Ombudsman as "the worst ecological disaster of the country" (*Clarín*, May 12, 2003). Engels's description of Manchester's Irk River might well apply, historical details aside, to the current state of this dead stream that defines an important part of the landscape of the Buenos Aires suburbs:

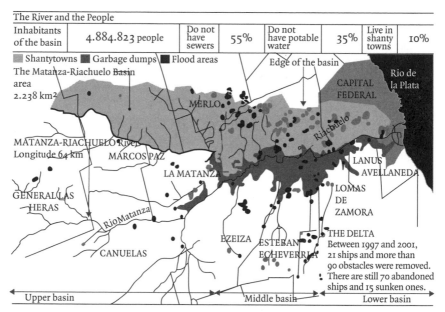

**Figure 1.1** *X-Ray of Matanza-Riachuelo Basin.* There are 4,884,823 inhabitants in the basin. Fifty-five percent of them do not have sewers; 35 percent do not have potable water; 10 percent live in shantytowns. Sewage waters, cesspools, and garbage (88,500 cubic meters are dumped each day) contaminate the river. There is also "industrial pollution." There are 3,036 plants in the basin (35 percent are food processing plants; 30 percent are chemical plants; 35 percent are cold storage, textile, metallurgic, and paper-manufacturing plants). The river has high concentrations of arsenic; chromium (38 micrograms per liter [2 micrograms per liter is considered "normal"]); mercury (5 micrograms per liter [0.1 micrograms per liter is considered "normal"]); and lead (16 micrograms per liter [1 microgram per liter is considered "normal"]). There are 140 garbage dumps in the area; 40 of them are illegal (*Clarín*, June 21, 2006).

A narrow, coal-black, foul-smelling stream, full of debris and refuse . . . [giving] forth a stench unendurable even on the bridge 40 or 50 feet above the surface of the stream. . . . Tanneries, bonemills, and gasworks, from which all drains and refuse find their way into the Irk, which receives further the contents of all the neighbouring sewers and privies. (Engels 1887 [1993]:62)

Less than a decade ago, Javier conducted ethnographic fieldwork in Villa Jardín, one of the largest shantytowns located in the flood zone adjacent to the Riachuelo and close to a huge open-air garbage dump. In the extremely unhealthy environment of Villa Jardín, its dwellers suffer high degrees of respiratory illnesses (such as asthma), gastrointestinal and parasitic diseases, and epidemic skin diseases (scabies, lice infestation). Bacteria and parasites are a common presence in the water that *villeros* drink, and as a result diarrhea is common among children and adults during the summer. During winter, bronchitis, angina, and pneumonia plague slum dwellers in Villa Jardín and in most shantytowns. As a physician in the shantytown's health center puts it: "There are the same germs, yet the conditions are different."[9]

Flammable sits right on the southern banks of the mouth of the Riachuelo, also known as a giant open-air sewer.[10] According to a Federal Ombudsman comprehensive report, this area of the Riachuelo has high concentrations of arsenic, cadmium, chrome, mercury, cyanide, and phenol (see Merlinsky 2007b). Most important for the story that unfolds in the following chapters, the mouth of the Riachuelo has excessive concentrations of lead.

In his wide-ranging survey *Planet of Slums*, Mike Davis asserts that "almost every large Third World city (or at least those with some industrial base) has a Dantesque district of slums shrouded in pollution and located next to pipelines, chemical plants, and refineries: Mexico's Iztapalapa, Sao Paulo's Cubatao, Rio's Belford Boxo, Jakarta's Cibubur, Tunis's southern fringe, southwestern Alexandria, and so on" (2006:129). The next two chapters will show why Villa Inflamable should be added to this gruesome list.

# 2

## The Compound and the Neighborhood

Flammable shantytown is located in the district of Avellaneda, right on the southeastern border of the city of Buenos Aires, adjacent to one of the largest petrochemical compounds in the country—Polo Petroquímico y Puerto Dock Sud. The Shell Oil refinery opened here in 1931.[1] Since then, other companies have moved into the compound. At the time of this writing, Shell refinery is the most important plant in the Polo. There is another oil refinery (DAPSA), three plants that store oil and its derivatives (Petrobras, Repsol-YPF, and Petrolera Cono Sur), several plants that store chemical products (TAGSA, Antívari, and Solvay Indupa among them), one plant that manufactures chemical products (Meranol), one dock for containers (Exolgan), and one thermoelectric plant (Central Dock Sud).

The name "Flammable" is quite recent. On June 28, 1984, there was a fire in the Perito Moreno, an oil ship that was harbored in a nearby canal. The ship exploded and produced what one elderly resident noted as the "highest flames I've ever seen." After the accident, companies in the compound built a new (and, according to experts, safer) dock exclusively for flammable products. The label "Flammable" carried over to the adjacent community—formerly known simply as "the coast."[2]

### Flammable Through Young Eyes

A year into our fieldwork, we provided a group of students at the local school with disposable cameras. We asked them to take half of the pictures of things they liked about the neighborhood and half of things they did not like.[3] Although a few of them stated that it was difficult to take pictures of the things they liked ("because there's nothing nice here..." "How can we take photos of the things we like if there's nothing pretty here?"), the concurrence among the groups was striking: among the things they like were people (most of the pictures classified by them as "good" portrayed friends and family) and institutions (pictures of the church, the school, the health center). Yet, even when

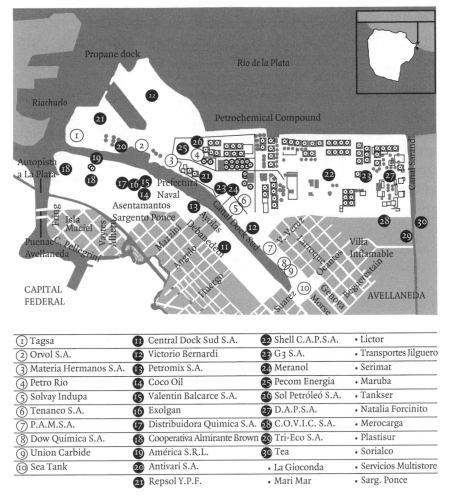

| ① Tagsa | ⑪ Central Dock Sud S.A. | ㉒ Shell C.A.P.S.A. | · Lictor |
|---|---|---|---|
| ② Orvol S.A. | ⑫ Victorio Bernardi | ㉓ G3 S.A. | · Transportes Jilguero |
| ③ Materia Hermanos S.A. | ⑬ Petromix S.A. | ㉔ Meranol | · Serimat |
| ④ Petro Rio | ⑭ Coco Oil | ㉕ Pecom Energia | · Maruba |
| ⑤ Solvay Indupa | ⑮ Valentin Balcarce S.A. | ㉖ Sol Petróleó S.A. | · Tankser |
| ⑥ Tenanco S.A. | ⑯ Exolgan | ㉗ D.A.P.S.A. | · Natalia Forcinito |
| ⑦ P.A.M.S.A. | ⑰ Distribuidora Quimica S.A. | ㉘ C.O.V.I.C. S.A. | · Merocarga |
| ⑧ Dow Quimica S.A. | ⑱ Cooperativa Almirante Brown | ㉙ Tri-Eco S.A. | · Plastisur |
| ⑨ Union Carbide | ⑲ América S.R.L. | ㉚ Tea | · Sorialco |
| ⑩ Sea Tank | ⑳ Antivari S.A. | · La Gioconda | · Servicios Multistore |
| | ㉑ Repsol Y.P.F. | · Mari Mar | · Sarg. Ponce |

**Figure 2.1** "The companies within the compound and Flammable" (Courtesy of Clarín)

they placed the school among the "good" pictures, during the interviews they did not fail to notice its dilapidated condition. Many of them took pictures of the health center and included them among the "good" pictures, but not for reasons they would consider worthy: they routinely use the center when they get sick or when there is an emergency. During our interviews, those who pictured the center stressed how well they are treated. Among the things they dislike, they all mentioned: the dispersed garbage and debris, the stagnant and filthy waters, the smokestacks, and the building of the main company within

**Photo 2.1** "The barrio, the wall, and the compound." (Photo taken by Javier Auyero)

**Photo 2.2** "Mi barrio." (Photo taken by Divina Swistun)

the petrochemical compound (Shell-Capsa). They all abhor the contamination of the water, the soil, and the air, and they emphasize that pollution is the only reason they consider leaving the neighborhood. Before we move to the pictures two forewarnings are in order. Note that we never mentioned pollution to them during the week we did the exercise; we told them we were interested in their views of their barrio. The issue of pollution is something they introduced in our conversations. Note also that it is not our purpose at this point to evaluate the truth value of their statements: whether the high-voltage wires or the coke plant causes cancer is not as important here as the fact that they resolutely believe this to be the case and that they grabbed the opportunity given by the proposed photographic exercise to express these beliefs. In other words, in what follows we simply want to introduce the reader to the physical space of Flammable (and, to the extent it is possible in a written text, to its sounds and smells) with the help of the images and voices produced by local youngsters.

### The "Good" Pictures: The (Few) Things They Like

Photos 2.3 and 2.4 (The Health Center): "There's an ambulance there, and they take good care of you." "If something happens, you can go there and they treat you very well."

Photos 2.5 and 2.6: "The school building is falling apart. It's damn cold in the winter, we can't attend classes because of the cold. If you turn the [electric] heating on, the lights go off. And in our classroom there's a broken window, and it's very cold (*nos recagamos del frío*)."

**Photo 2.3**

**Photo 2.4**

**Photo 2.5**

### The "Bad" Pictures: The (Many) Things
### They Don't Like

Overall, school students stress they didn't like the "bad" pictures because they show how dirty and contaminated their *barrio* is: "We don't like any of these pictures because there's a lot of pollution, a lot of garbage"; "I like

**Photo 2.6**

the neighborhood, all my friends are here. But I don't like pollution." In their minds pollution is associated with smoke (represented in the pictures of smokestacks, most of them taken late in the afternoon when the smoke can be better seen and thus excluded for their poor quality),[4] garbage, mud, and debris (represented in the pictures they took of the front of their houses, their backyards, and the streets they traverse daily). Pollution is also associated with the main company within the petrochemical compound and particularly with the coke processing plant that was installed a decade ago (environmental organizations and some community activists tried unsuccessfully to stop the opening of the plant, arguing that it was potentially carcinogenic).

Photo 2.7: "This is the street where Yesica lives."

Photo 2.8: "And this is in front of her house."

Photo 2.9: "This is right in front of our house. There's a man living there, poor guy . . . you feel sorry for him. The rats are all around."

Photo 2.10: "This is my aunt's backyard."

**Photo 2.7**

**Photo 2.8**

Photo 2.11: "This is my backyard."

All of them see themselves as living amid waste and debris, *en el medio de la basura*, surrounded by stagnant and stinking waters, and by refuse that feeds huge, menacing rats. In several conversations during our fieldwork, mothers told us that they feared their babies would be eaten by rats "which are this big!"

**Photo 2.9**

**Photo 2.10**

Photos 2.12 and 2.13: "When you walk by, the stench kills you...you can see the rats there, they are huge, like monsters." "Look at the river...it is all contaminated...I wish the neighborhood were cleaner."

Photo 2.14: "This is where we play soccer (in gym classes)....I wish it were cleaner."

**Photo 2.11**

**Photo 2.12**

One of the most revealing dialogues was the one we had with Manuela (who is now sixteen). One of the photos (Photo 2.15) she took shows the site where unmarked trucks dump garbage. Many neighbors scavenge in the garbage and, according to Manuela, "they make a lot of money." In Photo 2.16, probably the one that best encapsulates students' concerns about their dirty surroundings,

**Photo 2.13**

**Photo 2.14**

Manuela caught a cat eating from the garbage. And she uses the same word that she used to refer to her neighbors (*ciruja*, a scavenger): "Check out this cat... He is looking for something to eat. He is a scavenger cat (*un gato ciruja*)." One would hardly need sophisticated interpretive skills to realize that in matters of survival strategies and of surrounding dirt, neighbors and animals are, in Manuela's eyes, quite similar.

**Photo 2.15**

**Photo 2.16**

Pollution is not solely out there—in dirty streets, backyards, and play-grounds—but inside their own bodies where "contamination" has, in their view, a very precise name: lead. In 2001, an epidemiological study detected high levels of lead poisoning among young children in the neighborhood (see below). The study received a lot of media attention—in the written press, which school students don't read, and on TV, which they do watch. Teachers also inform them about lead, and some of them or their relatives were themselves tested for the study. When speaking about pollution, they used the interviews and the pictures to talk about their loved ones and themselves as *poisoned persons*: "I would like to leave because everything is contaminated here. I don't know how much lead my cousin has in his blood . . . all of my cousins have lead inside" (Laura). "I have lead inside. . . . I had my blood tested because some lawyers said they were going to eradicate us" (Manuela).

Photo 2.17: "We don't like the factories because of all the smoke."

Photo 2.18: "This is all polluted. It's all coming from Shell."

Photo 2.19: "I don't like Shell because it brings pollution. . . . I don't know how much lead we have in our blood."

Many of the students have visited Shell's plant (Photo 2.20). Miguel liked it; as he puts it: "It's really cool . . . full of trucks." Carolina, who took a two-week-long computing course inside the company's premises, says, "It is ugly inside, machines, smoke, lots of smoke." Romina tells us that she and others "don't like it [Shell-Capsa] because at night there's a lot of smoke coming out. We once went

**Photo 2.17**

**Photo 2.18**

**Photo 2.19**

to visit. They treated us really well, but they contaminate everything.... [Pointing to the coke plant] In front of my place, there's a woman who came to live to the neighborhood with her daughter. After a couple of years, they were all contaminated because of the coke.... Most people are contaminated by that." As Samantha puts it: "There's a lot of disease here (*acá hay mucha enfermedad*)."[5]

**Photo 2.20**

In the pictures they took and in the opinions they expressed in conversation, it became quite evident that these youngsters blame Shell (and the petrochemical compound by extension) for the smoke and the lead that affect their health. As they see it, Shell and the high-voltage wires (see Photo 2.21) that were put up in 1999 are the source of most of the community's health problems. As Miguel describes, referring to Photo 2.21, "These wires carry lots of watts. I've been told they are really dangerous. They bring skin cancer." Nicolás's picture (Photo 2.22) summarizes this generalized perception: "This picture shows what we don't like. The coke plant, the wires."

Many students took pictures of Dock Oil, an abandoned factory that was the site of the most recent community tragedy (see Photos 2.23 and 2.24). On May 16, 2005, three youngsters, one of them a classmate of the students we interviewed, broke into the premises of the abandoned building to scavenge for iron bars. Apparently, a wall fell down after one of the teenagers pulled the wrong beam. Two were injured, and the third died. When asked, the students were straightforward about the reasons why they included so many pictures of Dock Oil among the "disliked" aspects of their neighborhood: "Because that's where one of our classmates died," they all said. As we looked at the pictures and transcribed these youngsters' voices, we couldn't help but think that the reason they included so many pictures of that (ugly) building is related to the

**Photo 2.21**

**Photo 2.22**

shaky ground on which they live—both literally and figuratively. No image, and certainly no words, can better convey the sense of insecurity that, based on unsafe terrain, is widespread among these youngsters.

Where does this visual journey leave us? Youngsters' images and voices serve us well to introduce the reader into the physical and symbolic space of

**Photo 2.23**

**Photo 2.24**

Flammable. These lives do not unfold on the head of a pin but in polluted waters, poisoned soils, and contaminated air, surrounded by garbage where rats, as one of the students unambiguously put it invoking his worst nightmares, "look like monsters." Youngsters think and feel about the surroundings not as something to be occasionally reckoned with but as something oppressively present. To quote from Kai Erikson (1976), they see the environment as "a sample of what the universe has in store for them." In presenting a single, almost monolithic, point of view on their surroundings, these pictures and youngsters' critical comments misrepresent what is a far more complicated (confused and confusing) experiential reality.[6] Before getting into our main subject, let us reconstruct the history of Flammable with the help, this time, of older folks.

## An Organic Relationship

According to the last available figures, in the year 2000 there were 679 households in Flammable (Lanzetta and Spósito 2004; Dorado 2006). It is a fairly new population; 75 percent of the residents have lived in the area for less than fifteen years. Although there is no exact count, municipal authorities, community leaders, and people who live and/or work in the area (in the petrochemical compound, the school, and health center) told us that in the past decade the population increased at least fourfold—growth fed by shantytown removal in the city of Buenos Aires and by immigration from other provinces and nearby countries (Perú, Bolivia, and Paraguay). Internal differences divide Flammable into roughly three areas: the "barrio Porst" (for the name of one of the first inhabitants), the "barrio Danubio," and "la villa." The barrio Porst (also known by its inhabitants as "the bubble" or "these four blocks") is composed of old-time, lower-middle-class residents living right in front of the compound (where the local school, the health center, and the church are located). The barrio Danubio is located at roughly three blocks from the old core, also in front of the compound, but composed mainly by a group of twenty-two poor families living in very modest houses sitting right below a line of high-voltage wires installed in 1999. Our ethnographic work is focused mainly on these two areas. Residents of Porst and Danubio define most of the rest of the neighborhood as "el bajo" (the lowlands) or "la villa" (the shantytown). This sector is composed of poor dwellers (most of whom arrived in the last decade) who live in precarious houses, some of them in shacks located in the middle of swamplands.

These divisions are not merely geographic; they constitute organizing principles of the experience of place among old-time residents. Most of them believe that, with the increasing population in the shantytown, their barrio became unsafe. "The barrio was really pretty, now it is dangerous," we heard often. As García and Irma, a couple who have been living in the neighborhood for more than fifty years, put it:

Irma:    It was nice, but not anymore.

García:  No...not now. Now you have to lock yourself inside. You are always thinking that someone is going to mug you. You cannot leave anything outside.

Irma:    I live in fear, scared...they might kill you to get your TV....This was beautiful, it was peaceful.

García:  ...we didn't have gates in our home.

Or as Juan Carlos says, "We started to have problems because, with the new settlement, the quality of people changed...there're a lot of drugs, people who are not well-intended." For García, Irma, and Juan Carlos, as for many other old-timers, the depacification of everyday life is intricately related with the arrival of the shanty-dwellers. From the point of view of Danubio and Porst residents (poor and lower middle class alike), the "shantytown" is not only the repository of criminals but also of people who don't work and don't want to work, of people who don't pay taxes, and, most important for the purposes of the argument of this book, of people who are "dirty" (sucios) and "do not care much" (no se preocupan) about their hygiene. Given how crucial this aspect is to understanding the lived experiences of contamination, we will explore it in greater detail later; let us now simply highlight that the "villa" is seen by many old-timers as the place where contamination is located (by opposition, the "bubble" is not polluted). Despite the fact that lead-poisoned children are evenly distributed throughout the old and new parts of Flammable, many old-timers believe that lead belongs to the shantytown.

Flammable is, in many ways, similar to other territories of urban relegation in Argentina: it was deeply affected by the explosion of unemployment and the ensuing misery of the 1990s (Auyero 1999). Residents mostly subsist on part-time manual jobs in one of the companies of the compound, retirement pensions, scavenging, and state welfare programs.[7]

As in many other poor enclaves, neighbors have witnessed the dramatic and highly consequential increase in interpersonal violence in daily life. We recorded several instances of this during the course of our fieldwork:

*Fieldnotes (Débora), February 7, 2005*

Today, at 2.30 A.M. someone stole the phone wires. A neighbor saw the wire lines moving, and she passed the word to her neighbor who in turn told Chengo. He fired some warning shots into the air to scare off the thieves while others called the Prefectura (Coast Guard). The guys from Prefectura came later but said they could not get involved because "this is not our jurisdiction." A drunkard was sleeping in front of the grocery and the same thieves beat him up and stole his bicycle. My grandmother says that with all the stolen wires they can make up to 800 pesos. The thieves spread the word: "on the 10th Telefónica (the phone company) will put the wires up, on the 11th we'll steal them." My grandmother says that the police do not show up because they have a deal with the thieves: half (of the money) for the cops, half for the thieves.

### March 5, 2005

I came back at 4 A.M. As soon as I get out of the cab, my grandmother screams: "Get in quickly, people are shooting at each other." From my sidewalk I see my neighbor Jorgelina calling an ambulance. One boy is injured. I see him laid in the sidewalk. I get inside and my mum tells me: "You got here just in time! I was praying for you not to come. You could have been shot! They've been partying all night long. Nobody was able to sleep. You cannot return home at this time. From now on, you either come back before twelve or your stay overnight elsewhere" [ . . . ] I returned home only two minutes after the gunshots were over. Thank God I had to wait the cab for 40 minutes! Every day this neighborhood is becoming more dangerous.

### March 16, 2005

As I am waiting for Verónica, I see Josefina, a friend of my grandmother, coming to me, crying desperately and screaming: "Someone broke into my house, they robbed me, everything is upside down! They took my money, some gold stuff. . . . You should see my house. Everything is a mess." I try to calm her down. I ask her if she was there when the thieves broke in. No, she was having mate with my grand-aunt. While she is telling me this, two kids pass by. Josefina says: "Those are the thieves. They should be killed." Many neighbors get together. Isabel says that now that there are no more phone wires to steal, the thieves will begin to break into our houses. She then adds: "This cannot be possible . . . they should be shot down."

### March 27, 2005

When am I going to write something nice about the neighborhood? Every day is more complicated. . . . Today, over lunch my grandmother brought up the robbery at Josefina's. For the last two years or so, these subjects (robberies, etc.) are more frequent during lunch- and dinner-time. My grandmother tells me that Josefina's house was stoned on Thursday night. Apparently, the same thieves who broke into her home were throwing her stones. They were offended because Josefina called one of them "chorro" (thief ) when he stopped by her house to ask her how she was doing.

### January 17, 2006

At 3 A.M., gunshots. Apparently a neighbor fired some gunshots into the air to scare some kids who are trying to steal the phone wires that Telefónica put up yesterday. Personnel from Telefónica said that this is the last time they put the wires up, because the neighborhood is now a "red zone." Some neighbors are mounting guard during the night, saying that the wires will not be stolen again.

As a result of the routine theft of the highly prized copper wires, phone lines were repeatedly down. During the course of our fieldwork, this was a constant source of worry among residents, even among those few who were able to afford cellular phones (mainly used to receive but not to make calls). Lack of access to regular phones (and increasing daily violence) came to exacerbate an already present feeling of social isolation that pervades the lives of residents of Barrio Porst and Danubio—a feeling that stems from Flammable's marginal physical location and difficult access. Surrounded by the walled compound on the one side, and by a river and a canal on the other, Flammable sits literally on the margins of Avellaneda. Access to the neighborhood is quite difficult: There is one bus line run by a local family (the two buses run, not very reliably, every half hour from 6 A.M. to 10 P.M.); cabs habitually refuse to enter Flammable at night and occasionally during the day. As a result, residents have to shop locally, take an expensive car service to a chain supermarket, or walk close to forty-five minutes to one of Avellaneda's main commercial strips.

Increasing violence is quite common in poor communities throughout Buenos Aires. What distinguishes the neighborhood from other poor communities, however, is (a) the particular relationship it has with the main company within the compound (Shell-Capsa), and (b) the extent of the contamination that affects the area and its residents. Let us tackle both issues in that order.

The brick walls and the guarded gates that separate the compound (see Photo 2.25) betray the organic connection that, for more than seventy years,

Shell-Capsa has had with the community.[9] Together with the other companies in the compound, they all have attracted an eager workforce that came from the interior provinces (mainly the northeast and northwest parts of the country) to look for work in Buenos Aires.[10]

In the life stories we collected, older residents remember an abundance of work in the area. They also recall the lack of housing close to the compound and their strenuous efforts to build what initially were shacks in the middle of swamplands—still, today, there are lowlands in the center of the neighborhood. Hauling and spreading fill materials appears in old timers' narratives as a very important joint activity of those early days—and still is, according to our observations and the in-depth interviews we conducted with middle-aged residents. Health practitioners who work in the area say that one possible source of local contamination may be the very materials that people used and still use to fill in their plots, materials that are sometimes packed with toxic waste.

> **Fieldnotes (Débora), June 7, 2005**
> On my way to interview Morón, I saw little piles of debris in the sidewalk. A neighbor who was trying to smash the rocks to pieces tells me that some trucks charge 5 pesos per container. Other trucks, if they don't have a place to throw the debris, give it for free.

**Photo 2.25** "Shell behind the wall." (Photo taken by Javier Auyero)

The following are the main elements of what we term the "material and symbolic entanglement" between the neighborhood and Shell, or *la empresa* as residents call it. Historically, Shell provided formal and informal jobs for men, who worked in the refinery, and for women, who did domestic work (cleaning and baby-sitting) for the professional workforce. Old-timers not only worked for Shell but also used the health center in the compound, and the company provided drinkable water and pipes and other building materials. Less than a decade ago, Shell funded the construction of the health center in the neighborhood. This center employs seven doctors and two nurses and has a 24-hour guard and an ambulance, something that is quite uncommon in poor neighborhoods throughout the country. According to Marga, the president of the local improvement association, Shell has been a good neighbor in most respects:

> [Shell] always gave us a hand. Although they say it contaminates, Shell always helped. Whenever we needed them, they were always there . . . [helping] the school, the kindergarten, the improvement association, the church. They provided paint, building materials, shoes, clothing, even medicine and food for the local soup kitchens—many, many things. Shell always helped the improvement association. They built the health center, the chapel, the building where the kindergarten functions. Everything was done by Shell . . . every time they were needed they were here.

Marga's sister, Ana, whose son is lead-poisoned and who runs a *copa de leche*, a center of milk distribution in the neighborhood, echoes this sentiment: "We can't complain about Shell, it is the best company. They always help us." Others extend this positive evaluation to other compound companies. Back when the only available telephone was inside the compound, they were allowed to use it, and the companies would provide them with kerosene and other necessities. "The firms always lent us a hand," García says. Many residents contrast the companies' solicitousness with the neglect of the municipal government. As Roberto puts it: "The companies always helped us. The municipality never, ever, fixed a street or the sewage. See those cesspools over there: Shell made them, not the municipality. The government never did anything here."

Although Shell has automated many of its operations and is no longer the main employer in the community, it still provides jobs to residents young and old. Furthermore, Shell routinely grants funds for the local school in what a company engineer we interviewed called a "social performance plan." To name just a few of the activities and the goods that the company funds and distributes observed during the course of our fieldwork: a nutritional program for poor mothers with undernourished children that includes the distribution of food; computing classes for school students (held inside Shell's compound); windows, paint, and heaters for the school building; the end-of-the-year trip for graduating classes of the local school; T-shirts with the Shell logo for student soccer, volleyball, and handball teams; and toys for schoolchildren on Children's Day.

Through a community relations division the company seeks to enact what a former municipal official calls a "good neighbor policy."[11] Shell's presence undoubtedly distinguishes Flammable from other poor communities. Residents visualize it as the most important local actor, much more important than the local state, that is implicated—for some, deeply—in the affairs in the neighborhood. Most people we talked to would resort to la empresa if they had an urgent problem to be solved, such as finding building materials for their homes, a job, or urgent health care. Shell, in turn, has a public relations person assigned exclusively to deal with community affairs; during our fieldwork, this person was a Mr. Sieppe. Much like town companies in many places around the world, Shell has a somewhat paternal relationship with the people of Flammable—mainly with those living right across the compound, in the oldest part of the neighborhood. This relationship implies a modest interest in the fortunes of the community and a minor obligation to the people who live there.

## A Poisoned Place

While Shell and some of the other companies in the compound have created community relations programs in Flammable that do not exist in other poor neighborhoods, their industrial processes have also produced more environmental hazards than those present in other Argentine shantytowns.[12] Thus, Flammable is also different from other destitute neighborhoods throughout Buenos Aires in the extent (and known effects) of its air, water, and soil pollution. Experts from both the local government and Shell agree that, given the air quality associated with the industrial activities that take place in the compound, the area is unsuitable for human residence. As one industrial engineer who works at Shell told us: "This is an industrial area; people should not be living here."

The area bordering the compound has also been used as a dumping ground for many of the nearby companies (one large oil company was recently ordered to clean up a small fraction of it by the state government). It still used as an open-air waste disposal site for subcontractors who illegally dump garbage in the area; we witnessed several occasions of this during our fieldwork (see also Dorado 2006, and minutes from Comité de Control y Monitoreo Ambiental, June 26, 2003).[13] Oftentimes, as we noted above, residents pay to get the trucks to dump on their plots so that they can use the waste to fill their low-lying areas. In fact, in the many life histories we collected, filling with garbage seems to have been a common strategy in the neighborhood. As Ana recollects, referring to the plot in which her house stands now: "This was a lagoon. We fill it with all sorts of stuff, cement, stones, that black thing . . . we paid 5 pesos per truck." As in many other poor neighborhoods in Buenos Aires (Defensoría 2006), many of the pipes that connect homes to the city water supply are plastic; defects in the joints and breaks allow the toxins in the soil to enter the stream of the officially defined "potable water." The stench coming from these garbage disposal sites, from putrid waters filled with this same garbage, and from the chemicals stored and processed in the compound at times is nauseating. Stench is not easily captured in writing. In what follows we try to give a sense of what daily living in Flammable smells like by presenting a set of raw brief fieldnote excerpts. The excerpts also anticipate, in elementary form, some of the themes that will become central when we scrutinize the lived experience of pollution.

**Photo 2.26** "Dumping in Flammable." (Photo taken by Débora Swistun)

### Fieldnotes (Débora), January 8, 2005

I just came back home after a long day at work. It's really hot. As I am going to the bathroom to take a shower, my mother tells me: "Close the windows... don't you smell something? They are discharging something." The smell is sickening. As she is closing the windows, I tell grandmother to call the municipal ecological police....

I'm still inside. I don't know whether the smell is still out there. I can't smell a thing here. Every time there's this kind of odor we close everything; it is as if we are surrounded by decomposed garbage. After five minutes or so, my mom tells me that the smell is gone. She tries to convince herself by saying: "It might be the weather." "Yes," I reply, "it's Flammable's weather... the stinking smell of the *cinturón ecológico* [the name of the nearby landfill]."

### February 6, 2005 (Débora)

I just came back from my vacation at the beach. I needed a "change of air" (*un cambio de aire*). My nose was all full of mucus before leaving. Stuffy nose. While I was at the beach, I felt great. Clear nose. The air of the ocean did me really well. As the bus approaches the neighborhood, my nose is all clogged. It's really amazing. We can't live here anymore.

### January 15, 2006 (Débora)

I ask my aunt who is visiting us from [the northern province] Formosa if she felt anything when she first came into Flammable. "Yes," she answers, "a putrid smell." My cousin is also feeling dizzy.

### June 10, 2006 (Javier)

Every time I go to the neighborhood, I feel "slow..." Tired. I keep yawning every five or ten minutes. Today Débora noticed it and she asked me if I had a bad night. I replied that no, that I slept really well.

### January 20, 2006 (Débora)

(In the bus, coming back from La Plata) I smell rotten eggs as I approach the area.... As I come close, the odor is nauseating, intolerable. As seen from the highway, the neighborhood is covered by gray clouds.... I asked myself how many years of toxins are accumulated in those clouds. But I also wondered what's in my blood and in my lungs.

### February 10, 2006 (Débora)

My grandfather died today. At home, as he always wished, surrounded by his family. According to the doctors, it was a lung infection. He always had problems with his lungs during wintertime.... For many years he worked in [the oil company] Astra. As I saw him laying in bed I couldn't help but wondering whether or not contamination had anything to do with this.

An epidemiological study funded by the Japan International Cooperation Agency and carried out by an interdisciplinary team of experts compared a sample of children between seven and eleven years old living in Flammable with a control population living in another shantytown (Villa Corina) with similar socioeconomic characteristics but with less exposure to petrochemical waste and emissions. The study shows that, in both neighborhoods, children are exposed to chromium,[14] benzene (a known carcinogen for which no safe threshold exists), and toluene.[15] But lead, "the mother of all industrial poisons...the paradigmatic toxin [linking] industrial and environmental disease" (Markowitz and Rosner 2002:137), distinguishes the children of Flammable from the rest. The study shows that 50 percent of the children tested in the neighborhood have blood levels that exceed the level at which people are declared to be lead-poisoned (against 17.16 percent in the control population).[16] It also found that Flammable children had lower IQs and a higher percentage of neurobehavioral problems—both of which are symptoms of childhood lead poisoning. Flammable children reported more dermatological problems (eye irritation, skin infections, eruptions, and allergies), respiratory problems (coughs and bronchial spasms), and neurological problems (hyperactivity) than the control population. Children in the neighborhood also reported sore throats and headaches in higher proportions than the control population.[17]

## A Messy and Dangerous World

There is little doubt that the physical space in which Flammable residents carry out their daily lives is highly contaminated from past and present industrial activities (see Dorado 2006). Located southwest of the compound, Flammable is also adjacent to a huge (and, for practical purposes, unmonitored) landfill and to Tri Eco, one of the largest waste incinerators in the country.[18] How do residents perceive the surrounding danger and toxicity?

Adult residents seem to embrace Shell's vision of "total security" that, though technically unachievable (Perrow 1984), the company projects in its annual reports (see next chapter). Many of the men we talked to have worked inside the compound and say that, as one old-timer states, "there is plenty of control and safety" there. As Raúl puts it,

> There is no place in the world safer than that, no refinery in the country is as safe as this one. They have very sensitive alarms, double, triple alarms. If one fails, there's another one. If there's a gas leak, an alarm goes off, and everything is stopped. Even at the smallest problem, everything is stopped.

Similar to the ways in which the French nuclear peninsula analyzed by Françoise Zonabend (1993) is seen by its neighbors, the compound is perceived by many residents as "a world apart," as Marga put it. "Most of the time you have no idea what's going on inside." (Like every other person in the neighborhood we talked to, she doesn't know the number of firms located in the compound.)[19] Residents such as Raúl, however, are able to recognize the different sounds of the alarms—like those announcing a leak or a fire. Although they say that there's a permanent risk to living in proximity to the compound, residents don't really think about that possibility in their daily lives; the fact that the last serious accident, the explosion of the oil tank, occurred more than twenty years ago helps to normalize risk. When we ask them about the likelihood of an accident, we find an interesting convergence among people who otherwise diverge in their opinions regarding sources, extent, and effects of contamination. Almost every person tells us that in matters of industrial accidents, it does not really make any difference whether they live in Flammable or in some distant place:

> "If there's an accident here, half of the city of Buenos Aires blows up."

> "If something happens here, even if you are in Dock Sud [you'd be affected]"

> "Nobody will be safe if something goes wrong. Even if you are in [neighboring country] Uruguay . . . imagine, with all the tanks filled with combustibles, it would be as if 500 atomic bombs exploded at the same time."

> "If something happens there, everything in 50 kilometers around us is gone."

One could think of this convergence of opinions in two (not necessarily contradictory) ways: (1) people are deeply aware of the magnitude of the disaster that a serious accident can cause; (2) the devastation would be so widespread that it doesn't really matter that they live in Flammable. Interestingly, however, is the fact that when talking about the likelihood of accidents inside the compound, they are speaking of major catastrophes—like the explosion of the oil ship or the industrial disaster in Bhopal which was brought up a couple of times in conversations given that Union Carbide-Dow had, until 2007, a storage facility there. They are not thinking about countless minor accidents associated with the industrial activities that take place inside the companies (leaks, small fires, etc.) and that are intimately associated with the quality of air they breathe, the water they drink, and the ground on which their children and grandchildren play.

### The Clean and Safe Past, the Dangerous and Dirty Present

Environmental degradation was not suddenly imposed on Flammable residents. Unlike places that witness the sudden installation of a landfill, an incinerator, or a toxic industry in their proximity or whose members discover toxic assault through popular epidemiology, contamination in Flammable has been incubating since the compound was built. The Shell refinery opened seventy-five years ago on land that was not entirely vacant; Don Nicanor, one of the oldest residents, told us that his family used to live in what are now compound premises and was one day ordered to vacate.[20] Other chemical companies have been inside the compound for at least fifty years. The neighbors have been filling the swamplands since they first came here in the 1920s and 1930s, many times with soil and sludge coming from the compound—as Nicanor and others told us, the waste they used to fill the lowlands was packed with "all kinds of poisons." This slow incubation process is reflected in old-timers' narratives: nobody points to a moment in history where things made a turn for the worse. From a past filled with small farms and gardens, with fruits and vegetables that "smelled delicious," and with weekends at the nearby beach ("one of the most beautiful beaches in the entire country"), local families transitioned to a dangerous and dirty present. One day, they stopped going to the beach; another day they realized that the last farmer was gone.

It is interesting, however, to see the different ways in which they describe change; people who have been living in the same place, who are neighbors, friends, and/or relatives diverge in what they emphasize regarding the transformation of their living space. Some people highlight everyday violence as the main difference between present and past, others increasing contamination. While the increasing violence is usually traced to the expansion of the shantytown in what first used to be farmland and then a dumping site, the source of contamination of both the coast, where they used to go fishing and swimming, and the land, where they used to cultivate fruits and vegetables, is less clear. This lack of certainty about the origins of pollution is, as we will argue later, crucial to understanding their current experiences of contamination. Before we move into neighbors' recollections, one point of clarification is in order. It is quite probable that their memories are somewhat idealized, as Kai Erikson (1976:203) puts it, "partly because it is natural for people to exaggerate the standard against which they measure their present distress, and partly because the past always seems to take on a more golden glow as it recedes in the distance." We should take into account that usual idealization. We should also note that, paraphrasing Erickson, one way to convey the present uneasiness is to contrast it with a time and place that may have never existed in quite the form it is remembered, but the need to do this strongly indicates the depth of one's present discomfort.

García and Irma have been living in Flammable for more than fifty years; they came from the interior provinces when they were children. Whey they speak of how things used to be, the contrast with the present is stark:

I: There was this smell of flowers, fruits, wine, pears ... it was a spectacle. But everything is lost, there's nothing now ...

G: We used to cross the bridge [over the Sarandí River] and make a right. The first farm was there. They had peppers, this big! And the tomatoes were huge. What a perfume! There were pears, plums, grapes ...

I: And they made their own wine ...

G: They made salami ...

I: It was beautiful, it was beautiful ...

G: Nowadays, the coast is clean. But you can't go, they'll mug you, they would take your clothes off (*te asaltan, te desnudan*). Only thieves and drug addicts go there. . . .

I: My doctor tells me I should walk. But if you go there, they will mug you. If you walk here, it's full of trucks. So, I have to stay here, inside my house. You can't live like this.

Irma and García summarize an important part of old timers' feelings about the past—which are, as students of collective memory remind us, also experiences of the present. Although they do not put it this way, it is not hard to interpret the emphasis that most old timers put on the past smell of fruits and vegetables as a critical comment on the present stench of garbage and industrial pollution. The neighborhood became dangerous (and Irma and García are not alone in pointing at the recent slum relocation as the source of the trouble) but also busier and dirtier. Irma cannot go for a walk not only because of the thieves she thinks are looming everywhere but also because of the amounts of heavy-load trucks that traverse the neighborhood into the compound.[21]

Many other old-timers agree with Irma and García in their perceptions of the "beautiful" past and of increasing interpersonal violence, but disagree with the latter statement concerning the state of the coast. Morón, for example, remembers the coast as the place where "we use to go fishing, it was clean . . . now it's all putrid." He cannot pinpoint a time when he stopped going, but he knows why he stopped: it was dirty, oil spills were everywhere, and you could see dead fish lying in the beach. "That's because the ships clean their tanks near the coast, and the factories throw all their waste there."

In a dialogue with Raúl and Silvia, Débora relates her own family's experiences of the place.

> **Débora:** Did you go to the beach, because my grandmother told me that she used to go swimming . . . [Photos 2.27 and 2.28 portray Débora's family swimming in the nearby river.]
>
> **Raúl:** Yes, I went several times . . .
>
> **Silvia:** We went a couple of times . . .
>
> **Raúl:** But the last time, it was all dirty . . .
>
> **Débora:** Dirt . . . what kind of dirt?
>
> **Silvia:** Garbage, the things they throw out in the ports, grease, that black thing . . . like oil.

Ramiro's recollections of his first days in the neighborhood (he first came in the early 1960s) illustrate all the things that for him and for many a resident we spoke with are lost:

> There were few people . . . six or seven homes, all together. They were good people, *gente criolla*, everybody was working. At that time there was a lot of work, not like now, and *there were all first-class people*. . . . I saw the small farms, [they were] beautiful. I enjoyed working on my small plots a lot, I have lots of fruits there. . . . When I came with my nephews I asked them if they liked the place: "This is nice," they said. It was full of birds, thrushes, caracaras, storks. I am from Laguna de Iberá, in Corrientes. The place is quite a famous

**Photos 2.27 and 2.28** "Guada, Chichí and Rosario [Débora's relatives] enjoying the nearby beach, 1966." (from Débora's family album)

tourist site. And I liked it here because there were small lagoons. . . . In my plot I planted onions, melons, pumpkins. (our emphasis)

The farms, Juan Carlos says, were lost because of "contamination . . . the grapevines got dry because the soil and the water got contaminated. The only thing that remained for a while was the plum because it is more

**Photo 2.29** "Fishing in Canal Sarandí, 1960."

resistant." Every single old-timer remembers the farms, the lagoons, the fishing (see Photo 2.29) and contrasts that past with today's contaminated present.

Marga's recollections are some of the most detailed. They vividly illustrate another major change as seen from the eyes of old-timers: Together with increasing dirt and contamination, the arrival and growth of the adjacent shantytown is cited by old-timers as a major, if not the most important, change in *their* neighborhood:

Marga: When I was a kid, I went to play in the small farms. There were plenty of trees, we ate tomatoes from the *quintas* (gardens). Where the shantytown is located now, there were all *quintas*. It was beautiful, you have no idea how it was, it was beautiful.

Débora: And what happened with the *quintas*?

Marga: Well... [in the late 1950s] lowlands were filled with all the waste from the factories. At that time, the plants threw all the waste, the debris, here. And that's when the gardens began to go bankrupt. We use to play where the shantytown is now located, but before that it was called *la quema* (i.e., an open air dumping site). And then, everything began to get contaminated, and the factories here began to dump all the waste there, the gasoline, the tar, the coal. Whatever you can imagine, all the chemical waste was thrown there. . . . After all that waste, the land was useless.

Residents sometimes use the term "healthier" or "cleaner" to refer to a "safer" past—safer not only for its lack of pollution but for the absence of crime.

**Silvia:** It was healthier. My mother-in-law tells me that kids were allowed to go everywhere. Now if you let your kid play around, they [implicitly referring to shantytown dwellers] will bring him down there [the shantytown], and who knows what they will do to him. In the past, you could sleep with your door open, now you have to lock every single door and window. There's a lot of people you don't know.

Despite their dissimilar emphasis, however, their narratives contrast sharply with those of old-timers in other poor enclaves in Argentina (see, e.g., Auyero 2001). While depacification of everyday life dominates the experience of most middle-age and old residents across territories of urban relegation, Flammable residents differ from their poor counterparts elsewhere in emphasizing increasing environmental degradation: the present is not only a more dangerous place but a dirtier one that sometimes stinks.

This chapter began with a visual tour of Flammable as seen by its young residents. We then presented the objective side of environmental contamination. To approach the "subjective experience" of living in a poisoned place, we then proceeded to reconstruct the history of the neighborhood using the voices of its long-term residents. Pollution was not abruptly imposed on the neighborhood but developed gradually over the years. This slow incubation process, we will see, is very important for understanding the ways in which people understand toxicity. As we see in residents' reconstructions of the past, complaints about present contamination abound. But the next two chapters will show that beneath this general consensus lies a reality dominated by uncertainty about the sources and effects of pollution.

Pollution lives a double life: one in objective space—in the air, water streams, and soil of the shantytown; another one in the bodies and minds of contaminated inhabitants. To fully understand this subjective side of contamination, ethnographic observation is indispensable. Paraphrasing Wacquant (2007:9), we could say that ethnography is essential, first to pierce the "screen of discourses whirling around these [poisoned] territories of urban perdition which lock inquiry within the biased perimeter of the pre-constructed object" and second "to capture the lived relations and meanings that are constitutive of the everyday [contaminated] reality" of the slum dwellers. Our analysis will pay simultaneous attention to discourses that appropriate, transform, and/ or deny the toxic suffering of Flammable dwellers and to their everyday lived experiences. As we will soon see, both discourses and experiences are mutually imbricated.

# 3

## Toxic Wor(l)ds

### Karina's Suffering

Karina Olmos has been living in Flammable for twenty years. She lives in a precarious wood house whose garbage-filled backyard slopes downward into a filthy swampland. Unable to find a job (in the past, she had several as a cleaning person in some of the plants and homes inside the compound), Karina is one of the hundreds of thousands of beneficiaries of the Plan Jefas y Jefes state welfare program. She and her husband, Pedro (a car-service driver and also a beneficiary of the welfare program), are barely able to provide for themselves and their three children. Every Monday, Karina attends a workshop on nutrition that is funded by Shell for mothers of undernourished children. There, every month, Karina receives free food that, together with the state-funded soup kitchens where their children eat on a daily basis, help the household in making ends meets.

Luisa, Karina's eleven-year-old daughter, is lead-poisoned. According to a blood test she had two years ago, her lead levels are 18.5 micrograms per deciliter, far above what is now considered to be a nontoxic blood level of lead (10 μg/dl). That might explain Luisa's restless nights ("her sleep is jumpy," her mother says [*duerme sobresaltada*]), her random bouts of fever, and her occasional convulsions. "I told the doctor about the fever and the coughing," Karina says, "and the doctor told me that is because lead slowly consumes you." A year or so ago, an elderly neighbor died of saturnism, and Karina is scared for her daughter's health (*tengo miedo por mi hija*). The government-funded treatment for Luisa's lead poisoning was suspended more than six months ago and Karina does not know for sure when it is going to start again. If Luisa is to be cured, Karina believes, she has to go "on a treatment, take the medicine" (*así de la nada, no se va a curar*).

Karina thinks that her daughter "got contaminated by the factories" and points (to the best of our knowledge, wrongly) to the opening of the coke plant as the main culprit. Factories inside the compound, she notes, release particles that leave the clothes that she hangs out to dry all dirty: "Sometimes the smell coming from there kills you." A while ago, a lawyer told her that her kids were going to be examined for the effects of contamination, but she

**Photo 3.1** "Karina's house." (Photo taken by Javier Auyero)

**Photo 3.2** "Luisa playing with friend." (Photo taken by Javier Auyero)

has not heard from him yet: "I think there's going to be a lawsuit against the companies." Another lawyer is representing her and some of her neighbors in a lawsuit against Central Dock Sud, an electrical company that put up a high-voltage wire right on top of their homes. "They [the electrical company] are going to give us a house or money," Karina believes. She is hopeful about the outcome of the lawsuit and plans to move out of Flammable with the money she will receive. A doctor in La Plata, where she took Luisa for her lead treatment, told her that "the wires bring cancer." The lawsuit against the company, she tells us, seeks "the removal of the wires or our removal.... I don't know, we are waiting for the lawyer.... According to the lawyer, the Central Dock Sud should give us a lot of money."

During 2005 and 2006, Karina has been visited by many TV reporters seeking to put her daughter's story on the air. She bitterly complains about them, saying that they come "because my daughter has lead.... They show up, they promise help and then you never see them again. They use my daughter" (usan a mi hija). Journalists are not the only ones interested in her daughter. At the nutrition workshop, a representative of Shell asked for her permission to include Luisa's portrait in the 2005 company brochure that describes Shell's community promotion programs. When we talked with her in April of 2005, her two daughters had just developed skin rashes and pimples. "I don't know what to think," Karina told us, "I don't know if these [pimples] come from the wire, from the contamination, or from somewhere else." Because she has high blood pressure and chronic anemia, Karina herself is not feeling well: "I don't want to feel like this anymore because it is horrible."

Half a block from Karina lives her uncle, Francisco Olmos. He has been living there since the early 1960s. Now retired, after working as a contractor in many of the companies inside the compound, Francisco is completing the paperwork for his pension (though he does not know exactly when and how much he is going to be paid). He is also suing the electrical company but has not heard anything from the lawyer in a year. "They say we are going to get something like 50 thousand pesos," he said. When the local improvement association called for a meeting to discuss a possible relocation, Francisco did not attend: "I don't want to leave this place.... What if they put us in an apartment? We have a nice park here."

When asked about pollution, Francisco explicitly links the issue of contamination to government corruption. "Nobody is sure here" about pollution, he said. "I heard many things.... People say it's the coke plant, the one that is here inside Shell. But, if they knew that it was going to harm us, why did they [implicitly referring to government officials] give Shell permission to install it? That's because they [implicitly referring to Shell officials] gave money to [bribe] the mayor." Francisco is unsure about the true source and extent of contamination: "I raised three kids here. I myself have been inside many of the plants, and I don't have any [health] problems." One day, after a two-hour talk with Olmos about the history of the neighborhood, his son-in-law came in and, after listening to our conversation a few minutes, matter-of-factly asserted: "We are all contaminated here...with the coke plant and Shell, [we are] very contaminated [recontaminados]. We might not realize it, after so many years here, more than thirty. You think you are in good shape, but if you do a complete checkup..." Francisco disagrees with a smile: "I've been here forty-three years...I should be poisoned by now."

The Olmoses' story summarizes many of the central themes of our research: many residents are suffering the effects of living in a contaminated place; complaints about air, soil, and water pollution abound, but so do denial, confusion, and uncertainty about its extent and effects. The Olmoses' story also reveals that residents are not alone in their suffering and in their uncertainty. Doctors, lawyers, journalists, state officials, and Shell personnel, all part of the everyday life in Flammable, either propose their own definition of what the real problems (and attendant solutions) are, seek to broadcast residents' suffering (and its causes) to broader publics, (mis)diagnose their ailments and offer palliatives for their affliction, or promote dreamlike expectations about substantial compensations for present damage.

The coming chapters delve further into the lived experiences of contamination of Flammable dwellers: How do people make sense of toxic danger? Where does this collective understanding come from? Let us anticipate the main findings:

First, there are multiple, confused, and often contradictory points of view on the polluted habitat. There is also widespread blindness regarding sources and effects of toxicity. In what follows, we bring together all of these different points of view (and denials) without prioritizing one over the other. In this we seek to follow Bourdieu's method of presenting perspectives "as they are in reality, not to relativize them in an infinite number of cross-cutting images, but, quite to the contrary, through simple juxtaposition, to bring out everything that results when different and antagonistic visions of the (toxic) world confront each other" (1999:3). We will try to reproduce what, for us, is the defining, and most perplexing, characteristic of the experience of contamination in Flammable. Against simplistic and one-sided representations (created from the outside, mainly by the media) that construct this place as inhabited by people who think and feel about toxicity in a single, monolithic, way, our ethnography reveals a diversity of coexisting views and deeply held beliefs. Rather than being a determined, cohesive crowd up in arms against toxic assault, Flammable is dominated by doubts, lack of knowledge, and errors. Flammable's toxic experience is also characterized by divisions ("they," the shantytown dwellers are the ones who are really polluted) and a seemingly endless waiting time: waiting for judges to make decisions that will presumably award residents with hundreds of thousands of pesos in compensation, waiting for state officials to proceed with relocation, and waiting for companies to evict them.

Second, toxic uncertainty stems from (a) the very nature of pollution: the sources of contamination in Flammable are multiple and, in the case of specific toxic substances, unknown; (b) the multiple discourses and practices of actors that intervened in this space (from state officials to private lawyers, from activists to doctors, from Shell to the media), which amount to a veritable labor of confusion; (c) the relational anchoring of risk perceptions and, related, the history of the residents of Flammable, who many times use their own—to them, healthy—bodies to rebuff the very existence of contamination, displacing it either to the adjacent compound or to a nearby shantytown; and (d) the constant threat of eviction or relocation which, by itself, introduces a powerful source of uncertainty. Far from being a normal consequence of imperfect knowledge, the perpetuation of ignorance, mistake, and doubt is thus a "political consequence of conflicting interests and structural apathies" (Proctor 1995:8). In what follows, we seek to present the various points of view on contamination in Flammable and then explain their sociopolitical rationale.

## The Categories of the Dominant

When, more than three years ago, we began to do background research for this project, Javier contacted Isabel Corduri, a Shell public relations representative. Over the phone, very politely but firmly, she said, "Five years ago, before the people from the Villa 31 were relocated from the Capital Federal into Flammable, this place was very safe. You could go out at 2 A.M. as if you were walking in New York City at 2 P.M..... Nowadays, the personnel at the refinery have to go out with a private security escort." The reports published in the printed media regarding the contamination in Flammable "are all lies," she said. "We don't even waste our time answering them." When asked about the lead contamination described in the Japanese International Cooperation Agency (JICA) report, Corduri was conclusive: "Shell does not use lead." She then asked us for a list of specific questions to direct us to the right person but added that the person in charge of environmental matters had recently retired "and now this issue is coordinated from Brazil." The technical personnel are "very busy," she said. "I doubt they have time for you."

Somehow, Javier managed to get an interview with Axel Garde, Shell's manager of health, safety, environment, and quality, an industrial engineer who had worked at Shell for many years; the fact that Javier lives in the United States and works at a research university there may have helped. We doubt he would have made time in his busy schedule to talk to a neighbor like Débora, despite her academic credentials as an anthropologist. Garde's impression of the relationship between the company, the compound, and the neighborhood may offer the best possible synthesis of the way Shell sees the neighborhood and its residents. Garde did not want the interview to be tape-recorded despite the fact that, during the course of the two-hour-long dialogue, he complained bitterly that journalists routinely distort his statements. What follows is an edited version of Javier's fieldnote diary:

### *Fieldnotes (Javier), July 8, 2005*

After reading the two JICA reports, hundreds of pages of interviews with neighbors, and many news accounts, I finally made my way into Shell. Axel Garde told me via email that I should call a special car service. They know their way into the compound, there's an issue with "safety" here, he wrote.

This is the first time I go to Flammable in a car service. The driver from the car service company knows the way. "We work for Shell; we drive people in and out of the compound every day." The driver also told me that the cars that go from the city into the compound are different from the ones (such as the one I used on my way back) that are waiting outside the compound in Flammable. "These," he says referring to the car in which we are driving to the compound, "are brand new. They keep the beat-up cars there [right outside the compound] because . . . well, it's the shanty-town, you never know." The driver anticipates what I will hear from Garde: despite the intense relationship between *el barrio* and *la empresa*, these are perceived as two separate worlds, one safe and secure (Shell), the other one dangerous and contaminated (the neighborhood).

I cannot help but noticing Garde's shirt. It has the logo of a polo team—usually a sign of high-class belonging. Throughout our long conversation, Garde mixes perfectly pronounced English terms with Spanish; and he seems very familiar (sometimes even more knowledgeable than I am) with U.S. societal and political affairs.

It doesn't take long for us to get into what brought me here: environmental contamination coming from the compound. Concerning pollution, Garde is conclusive (if somehow contradictory). On the one hand, he repeats that the area where Flammable is located is "not fit for human residence because it is an industrial zone." On the other hand, he also says that "Flammable residents have no problems that are associated with industrial activities. The problems the neighborhood has are those associated with poverty: drugs, alcohol, etc." "Here," Garde asserts, "everybody emphasizes what's inside the petrochemical compound. But they don't realize what's in their homes: car batteries, garbage. . . . Contamination doesn't come so much from industrial activity but from the way in which people live their lives . . . . The neighbors don't know what they have in their surroundings. Lead is in every shantytown. It is not exclusive to Flammable. Lead has to do with poverty, with the fact that they [the poor] get a hold of what they have around them, for example they recycle car batteries . . . . Lead is not in the shantytown. Shanty dwellers bring it into the shantytown because they go out to scavenge, they fill their plots with rubble" (my emphasis). Over the course of the conversation, Garde comes back time and again to the *shanty dwellers' own practices as the main cause of contamination*: "Take the water, for example. It is contaminated because they hooked up to the main source illegally and these are lowlands. That's why the water is contaminated."

Garde makes a clear distinction between the old neighborhood, which (with no little amount of class irony) he calls the "área premium," and "la villa." The residents of the premium zone "have a right to live there because they are the owners"; the residents of the shantytown, on the contrary, "have no rights. They are now waiting for the indemnification that is going to come when they are relocated. But they don't want to leave because they live 5 minutes away from the capital." He then brings up the JICA report in relationship to the shantytown asserting that its dwellers want to profit from its results: "They see the possibility of doing business." This assertion leads him into a critical evaluation of the work conducted by JICA. He says that the air monitoring report (known as

JICA I)[1] was a "serious study. It did not demonstrate a thing [concerning air pollution]." JICA II, in turn, "is completely void [*nulo de nulidad absoluta*, he says]. It has many, many mistakes. Among them, the lead issue." He then elaborates on what he sees as the true source of lead and other toxins: not the environment but the behavior of shanty dwellers. "Lead is an illness of poverty, an illness of the guy who scavenges garbage.... The toluene they found may come not from the environment but from the medicine people take, from the preservatives contained in the soda they drink. Benzene, to take another example of what JICA found, does not come from industrial activity but from the fact that people there smoke and burn wood to heat their homes."

As we are concluding our conversation, Garde says that, "Neighbors know that Shell is not the problem," and then brings up the issue of Shell personnel as the best example of the way in which the company cares for the environment—something that is repeatedly asserted in Shell's annual reports. Workers here "are not affected, we control them periodically." And then, in a statement that I heard many times from old-timers in Flammable, he adds: "I am not affected either, *toco madera*, and I've been here twenty-five years." Not without a condescending tone that comes from his superior technical knowledge, he wraps up stating: "You need to distinguish the 'facts and findings' [he speaks the words in English] from the political interpretations. There are technical arguments and there are emotions. I rely on facts and findings, the rest is all politics."[2]

### Shell's Public Image: Safe and Responsible

Shell's annual reports (published in glossy colorful hard copies and also available at the company's Web site) project a positive public image. A number of phrases are repeatedly invoked in three reports (2001; 2002–2003; 2003–2004): sustainable development, corporate social responsibility, and protection of the environment and of future generations.

In a section titled "How Would We Like to Be Perceived (*Como queremos que nos vean*)" under the heading "The Image of Shell," the 2001 report asserts that "Shell CAPSA strives to be a leader in economic, environmental, and social terms" (49). Under the section titled "Our Commitment with Health, Safety, and the Environment," we read: "In the company we are committed to pursue the objective of causing no harm to people, to protect the environment...to achieve a performance that will make us proud in terms of health, safety, and the environment, to obtain the trust of clients, stock-holders, and society in general, to be a good neighbor, and to contribute to sustainable development" (50).

Two themes in the reports command our attention: the ways Shell deals with JICA's potentially damaging study; and the ways the company frames its policy toward the surrounding community. With regard to the JICA study, the three annual reports are consistent. In 2001, as the air monitoring quality is beginning to take shape, Shell's report details the different gas emissions produced by the refinery ($CO_2$, $SO_2$, $NO_x$) and carefully itemizes their progressive reduction (every yearly report thereafter documents this yearly reduction). In a section titled "Air Quality," the 2001 report refers to the measurement of air pollutants that is being conducted by the local municipality, the secretary of environmental policy of the state of Buenos Aires, the secretary of environmental policy and sustainable development of the federal government, and the government of the City of Buenos Aires. After informing that Shell lent its own mobile air monitoring station to collaborate with the study, the reports states that, in terms of the basic contaminants included in the monitoring, the median values obtained are within legal parameters of environmental quality (27).

In the 2002–2003 report, the section titled "Buenos Aires Refinery and Dock Sud Petrochemical Compound" states: "At Shell we are the first to be interested in the effectiveness of environmental controls because we are a company that operates in a responsible way, observing the standards set in the national legislation and those set by the Shell group which in many cases are even more demanding." After describing (as the 2001 report does) the international certifications that Shell has been awarded for its environmental performance and the investment the company has made to improve safety and protection of the environment, the report addresses the JICA epidemiological study (conducted during early 2003) and affirms that: "The disposal of lead, while it was utilized in the production of gasoline, was absolutely safe. Shell CAPSA never buried organic lead. There is no possibility whatsoever of finding metallic lead among the gas emissions of the Shell refinery" (10). The report then reiterates the lending of the mobile air monitoring station and ends: "Shell understands the concern of the Dock Sud community who legitimately seeks answers to a situation that worries it. We agree in the need to have access to extensive, transparent, and trustworthy information about the monitoring plan" (10).

The 2003–2004 annual report features an (almost identical) paragraph pertaining the JICA study. After stressing the need to clarify certain "technical matters," the report states that the "disposal of organic lead residues that were used in the making of gasoline up until 10 years ago was absolutely responsible and done according to accepted local and international practices" (21).

With respect to what Garde defines as "social promotions plans," the reports are also unfailing in its portrayal of a company that deeply cares for its neighbors. On page 45 of the 2001 annual report, in a section titled "Programs with the Community," the report describes the company's "open-door policy" in the Buenos Aires refinery along these lines: "In Shell we understand that the commitment with sustainable development requires an active corporate participation in the community and in civil society. Our attitude in favor of an open-door policy emerges from that understanding." The report then describes the weekly guided tours that the refinery organizes for local schools and community associations. Along these lines, the report features a subsection titled "Consultation with Our Neighbors" in which the company praises itself for its superior image: "Research conducted in our refinery's zone of influence allowed us to know the neighbor's perceptions regarding Shell CAPSA's operation.... The residents think of Shell as the company with the best image among those located in the area. Shell is considered [to be] the company that provides the best help to the neighborhood" (46). This help comes in the form of "investment activities in the community" that the different reports describe in detail because these activities constitute one "way of exercising corporate social responsibility. It is an investment with benefits on both sides: for the company and for the community. An example of this takes place in the Buenos Aires refinery...together with fueling the industrial growth in the area for more than 70 years, Shell is committed with the development of the local community...carrying out multiple initiatives with the objective of improving the infrastructure of the area and promoting the welfare of the neighbors" (47). The 2002–2003 annual report acknowledges the deep economic crisis of 2001 in the following terms: "During these times, the social aid ceases to be an option for the company and becomes an unavoidable duty" (53), and then reports the distribution of funds in, among other places, Flammable's local school (Escuela no. 67) and health center (San Martín de Porres). Shell's 2003–2004 annual report lists the new "social investment activities" (among them, the social promotion programs carried out under the name of "Creating Links" in Flammable described below) and remarks that "community organizations recognize the economic effort of the firm, but also appreciate the 'personal link' that Shell has established with them" (43). Shell's public image is thus that of a company that is responsible and safe and that cares for its neighbors.

### Scrutinizing Corporate Logic

Back in the United States, Javier began to research the existing knowledge concerning the relationship between oil refineries and lead. Wilma Subra, who serves on a number of U.S. Environmental Protection Agency national advisory committees, was kind enough to provide historical information and a larger sense of context: "Refineries that did produce leaded gasoline [as Shell did until 1995] have contaminated soils in the area with lead. A great deal of lead buildup in the soil is from historic air emissions. The lead has been related to elevated lead levels in children as well as high lead levels in mothers' milk. Until the contaminated soils and sludge are cleaned up, the lead will continue to impact the community." This statement succinctly captures the vast literature on the effects that the operation of a lead refinery has on the surrounding environment and, in particular, on lead contamination (Huntley, Bonnevie, and Wenning 1995; Croudace and Cundy 1995; Marcantonio, Flowers, and Templin 2000; Iturbe et al. 2006).[3]

We also learned that, as part of their routine operations, oil refineries release massive amounts of sulfur dioxide, volatile organic compounds, particulate matter, nitrogen oxides, and carbon monoxide. These pollutants form ground-level ozone and haze.[4] We then had a follow-up exchange with Garde via e-mail, and he once again challenged any link between the past activities of the refinery with the presence of lead in Flammable's environment. He asserted that: (a) refineries did not produce lead emissions, only vehicles that used leaded gasoline did; (b) when leaded gasoline was produced, sludge was incinerated or "treated with potassium permanganate and then immobilized with cement in pits"; (c) no responsible refinery places sludge in nearby land, (d) the area of Flammable "never was a dumping site for garbage, sludge, or other stuff coming from the compound, specially from our refinery. Debris of unknown origins was brought to the area by clandestine trucks or by the residents themselves who are scavengers. There are also people who brought rubble or garbage to level their plots. This filling can have all sorts of things, but not produced by the compound but by the lack of state control"; (e) the water pipes are all clandestine and have plenty of defects, and since they snake through a land filled with all sorts of debris (*llenas de inmundicia*), it is not hard to understand how people become poisoned. It is a "vicious cycle." To conclude, he wrote, "The refinery and the factories in the compound have nothing to do with the conditions of extreme poverty and the total lack of hygiene in which these people live. These people should *not* live there, they were brought here by misery and by political interests" (his emphasis).

Even after two years of reading the literature on environmental health and on environmental justice movements, and after consulting experts on the subject, we are ill-prepared to confirm or dispute Shell's assertions. And the main reason for that is that the government bodies in charge of controlling and regulating the activities of the compound industries (and of producing independent knowledge about them) are largely absent: Most of what we know about Shell comes from the company itself. A former undersecretary of the environment in the municipality of Avellaneda (where the compound is located) and currently undersecretary of environmental policy of the state of Buenos Aires told us so. In terms of what goes on inside the compound, he said, there's a complete lack of state information and control. In an interview in July 2006, the current secretary of environment of Avellaneda told us that more than 80 percent of the chemical products used in Argentina enter through (and are stored in) compound premises. She admitted that she did not know which products those were. Furthermore she acknowledged that the waste produced when the storage tanks are cleaned and the gases that these tanks emit go unmonitored. Accordingly, we just cannot know whether Shell's version regarding emissions and disposition of sludge is or is not true because no state agency supervises its activities. Despite this crucial limitation, let us start by doing what Shell's engineer suggests us to do, that is by separating "facts and findings" from "interpretations." We are here interested in scrutinizing Shell's position logically. The reason for doing so will become clear later: many residents in Flammable agree with Shell's perceptions and evaluations.

First and foremost: What do we know about lead? Research on sources and effects of lead is quite vast (for overviews, see Berney 2000; Warren 2000; Markowitz and Rosner 2002; Widener 2000). Lead in the environment results from the use of lead in industry. Lead accumulates in the human body (in the blood, tissues, and bones) in proportion to the amount of lead found in the environment. It can cause a vast number of health disturbances; according to the U.S. Environmental Protection Agency, effects range "from behavioral problems and learning disabilities, to seizures and death."[5] It is a poison that affects the brain, kidneys, and the nervous system in many subtle ways even at low levels (on the historical shift of what are considered "normal" blood lead levels, see Berney 2000 and Widener 2000). Extremely high exposure to lead can "cause encephalopathy and death, lower doses cause severe retardation, and lesser doses lead to school problems, small but significant shifts in IQ, and other measures of central nervous system function" (Berney 2000:205).

Second: Where does the lead come from? JICA I and II are inconclusive. But the reports give some hints: Lead in the air of Flammable (2.5 µg/m³) is higher than the state threshold levels (1 µg/m³). The small river (Arroyo Sarandí) that borders the shantytown is also contaminated with lead (and chromium). In May 2001, Greenpeace "took a sample in the immediate surrounding of (the hazardous waste incinerator) Tri Eco...the sample revealed the presence of high levels of lead, cadmium, chromium, copper, and zinc in the sediments associated with the discharge of effluents" (Greenpeace 2001). Experts we interviewed also point to the chemicals buried in the ground on which the children play and through which water pipes run as another possible source of lead poisoning. Almost every other old-timer in Flammable remembers stopping trucks coming from *inside* the compound (nobody was able to point to a particular company as owning the trucks, however) and ask them to dump its contents in their backyards in order to level their plots. Experts, furthermore, told us that for a long time before laws regulating toxic waste disposal even existed, the companies within the compound used Flammable as a free dumping zone. A case in point is YPF, the formerly state-owned oil company, which a few years ago was ordered to clean up an area in Flammable where "residues of the refining process were dumped."[6] Lead, in other words, might be coming from everywhere, from past and present (both uncontrolled) industrial practices.

Third: Where was lead found? Although lead poisoning and poverty are indeed related, not every poor enclave is equally affected by lead. On this, JICA II is conclusive: as described before, Flammable residents are more exposed to lead than are residents of an equally poor neighborhood elsewhere. What about differences *inside* Flammable? Are the cases of lead poisoning all in the shantytown part of Flammable? We were able to access the original data set culled by JICA II experts. Contrary to Shell's assertions, there is no evidence of clustering of lead cases within the shantytown area of Flammable. It is simply not true that lead poisoning is a shanty problem. Nor is, for that matter, the assertions concerning the cases of benzene intoxication: the JICA study controls for smokers and use of wood heaters. This, of course, does not prove that Shell responsible; it simply casts factual doubts about technical assertions.

We do not want here to engage in the logic of the trial. Let us simply point out how surprised we were when, reading the history of "deceit and denial" of the U.S. lead industry (Markowitz and Rosner 2002), we found striking rhetorical parallels between Shell's claims concerning the location of lead poisoning and the practices that cause it with those of the lead industry in the United States. Interestingly, both Shell and the lead industry point to the slums as the repository of lead and to the behavior of slum dwellers as the cause of their poisoning. According to Markowitz and Rosner, the first documentation of childhood lead poisoning in the United States dates from 1914 when a boy from Baltimore died "from white lead paint bitten from the railing of his crib" (2002:42). At the time, the lead industry and its defenders engaged in a "blame-the-victim" argument. They asserted that

> the real "culprit" was the child. They were able to do so because in the 1920s many viewed a child's lead poisoning as the result of pathological behavior on the part of the child. Some of the physicians reporting cases of lead poisoning in children described the poisoning as a consequence of another condition, pica, which as often considered an abnormal craving for nonedible substances; to make such a diagnosis put the child's own behavior in question, for pica was often associated with mental retardation. (43)

Lead, according to the industry, did not cause the children to be subnormal; children with pica, which caused them to chew on inedible (leaded) articles, were subnormal to begin with. In the case of workers, the lead industry blamed their personal hygiene practices for their elevated blood-lead levels. As Markowitz and Rosner assert, "The industry had long faulted personal habits such as fingernail biting, unwillingness to shower, general slovenliness and particularly a resistance to hand washing, and an affinity for dirty clothes among the industrial workforce as the 'true' source of lead poisoning" (139). This "blame-the-victim" strategy lasted long. In the 1950s the main trade group, the Lead Industries Association of America, was still reacting to reports of children sickened by lead by blaming the victims. In 1956, an article on childhood lead poisoning appeared in *Parade* magazine. Manfred Bowditch, the lead association's director of health and safety, told his predecessor, Felix Wormser, that he was concerned about the public relations aspect of such press accounts.

> [Bowditch] remarked that "aside from the kids that are poisoned...it's a serious problem from the viewpoint of adverse publicity." The basic problem was "slums," and to deal with that issue it was necessary "to educate the parents. But most of the cases are in Negro and Puerto Rican families, and how," Bowditch wondered, "does one tackle the job?" ... *"The problem of lead poisoning in children will be with us for as long as there are slums."* (2002:103, our emphasis)

Fifty years later, childhood lead poisoning is still being seen as a problem of the slums and as a result of slum dwellers' practices, not as a consequence of the lead-saturated environment in which they live. In what resembles the long discredited (at least in anthropological and sociological circles) "culture of poverty" argument, the dominant tells us that poor and dominated people become poisoned with lead because of their own careless behavior.[7] Interestingly enough, this same logic surfaced in the immediate aftermath of the Bhopal industrial disaster. Soon after large quantities of methyl isocyanate (MIC) escaped from the Union Carbide plant, company officials attributed the large number of deaths caused by the lethal chemical to the victims' behavior, emphasizing that those who ran or who did not cover themselves were at greater risk of exposure (Das 1995). This argument was later complemented by an equally offensive biological one.[8] As Das (156) writes, this line of reasoning said

> that most of the victims were suffering from malnutrition or a previous disease, such as tuberculosis; hence it was not possible to distinguish between a disease caused by the inhalation of MIC from that which may have resulted from a combination of factors, such as history of lung disease. This was like saying that because human beings were not like laboratory animals, the toxic insult to their bodies by the inhalation of methyl isocyanate—about which science did not possess definite knowledge—could not be decisively linked to the diseases encountered. One might even rephrase this to mean that those whose lives were already wasted by poverty and disease could scarcely claim just compensation merely on account of this further exposure to industrial disaster. This professional transformation of the experience of suffering, guilefully encoded in the language of science, ended up blaming the victim for his suffering.

Parallel discursive strategies aside, we focus attention on the assertions concerning location and cause of lead poisoning made by Shell personnel because they, in ways that will be seen shortly, are echoed in Flammable residents' categories of perception and evaluation. Different criteria, sometimes coexisting in the same individual, organize residents' views and judgments regarding the compound, the company, and their own neighborhood. Some of them believe, as Garde glibly asserted, "that Shell is not the problem." The real source of contamination is the shantytown and its dwellers. Others, while displacing pollution to the nearby *villa*, are less certain about Shell. And they somehow seem to know that, even if Shell has its share of responsibility, there's nothing you can do, as an old-timer told us, "against

**Photo 3.3** "Shell is everywhere in the neighborhood." (Photo taken by Javier Auyero)

that monster." Others still are less doubtful; as seventeen-year-old Samantha candidly told us: "Shell is making us sick." Before delving further into the poisoned points of view (or lack thereof) let us concentrate in another instance of the dominant discourse—an instance that is quite revealing because of what it hides.

### Let's NOT Talk about Lead

Shell is everywhere in the neighborhood: in the trucks that come in and out, in the logos of children's T-shirts, in the many "special programs" that the company funds in the neighborhood. Karina Olmos, whose story opens this chapter, was attending one of these programs at the local school (a nutrition program named "Let's play to eat well") when one of the coordinators asked her permission to include pictures of Luisa, Karina's daughter, in the catalog that Shell was producing to advertise its social promotion programs. "But Luisa has lead..." Karina hesitantly replied. That was not considered a problem by the social worker. Karina signed a consent form, and a few months later she received the catalog.

It is a superbly produced forty-page, full-color catalog that contains several glossy pictures of Luisa playing in swings of the local school plaza, reading, and smiling, always smiling for the camera (Shell-CAPSA did not authorize us to reproduce the catalog's images here). The cover of the catalog reads: "Lessons Learned. Shell and the Community. Contest of Social Projects 2003–2004." It opens with a letter from Shell-Argentina's president, Juan José Aranguren, in which he highlights the "active policies" that Shell puts in place to strengthen the relationship between the company and the community where it operates. The catalog presents, describes, and evaluates the program "Creating Links" which comprise twenty "social projects" that were partially funded by Shell. The main objective of the program, reads the catalog, is to "contribute to improve the quality of life of children and adolescents living in conditions of poverty and exclusion in Avellaneda" (7). The program focused mainly in the "most critical zone of Avellaneda: the zone commonly referred to as Villa Inflamable" (7). The total number of beneficiaries of the program, according to the catalog, is 4,042 persons, mostly children and adolescents ranging from five to seventeen years old. The total investment was US $88,000, of which 30 percent (roughly US $29,000) was contributed by Shell (according to its annual report, in 2004 Shell invested US $6,700,000 in the Dock Sud refinery). Implicitly acknowledging the relatively paltry sum, the catalog stresses that "economic resources are not always the most important element in a social program. Human resources, impossible to quantify, made the difference in the value added during this job" (7). The catalog ends with several reflections on the social responsibility of the business world and a call for strengthening the relationships between business, organizations of civil society, and the community—reflections that apparently emerged from the experience of "Creating Links."

On page 14, the catalog describes one of the projects carried out in Flammable's local elementary school. A picture of school kids playing in the colorful swings of the school park heads the page where the project "Opening Roads" is described in detail. The activities carried out under this initiative, reads the catalog, were three: 1. Construction of the nearby plaza, 2. Painting of the school patio, 3. Fixing classrooms and general infrastructure. Among the achievements of this initiative, the catalog lists: 1. The school infrastructure was improved. 2. The new plaza was opened, and more safety was provided to the local school.

The plaza is, in fact, in the state of abandonment shown in Photos 3.4 and 3.5. There are no swings, the slide is broken, and the rest of the features that appear in the catalog (even the small tree!) are gone. We are not

**Photos 3.4 and 3.5** "School playground." (Photos taken by Javier Auyero)

implying corporate bad faith: we do not think (and we have no evidence to sustain such a claim) that the catalog was a montage to cover the real conditions in which children and adults live in the neighborhood. We are bringing up the different plazas (one image for consumption among the business world; the other, the real one, for local use—or, given its sorry state, lack thereof) because, we believe, they reveal a general trend present in the actions, words (and in this case, images) that Shell broadcasts about the neighborhood and its inhabitants. Everybody involved in the production of the catalog (from the social workers and teachers involved in the on-the-ground operation of the program, to the general coordinator of "Creating Links" and the photographers and designers assigned to produce the catalog) might have had the best intentions—to do well, to improve the living conditions of Flammable poor. We have no reason to believe otherwise. And yet, a catalog that so completely misrepresents the actual material conditions in which children live and play discloses the denial of which Shell (and, as we will see, many other institutional actors) is part and parcel. Can the many pictures of smiling and playing lead-poisoned Luisa (with no mention whatsoever of her fragile condition) mean otherwise? In a catalog that emphasizes its concern for "sustainable development," can the fact of lead-poisoned young bodies be so completely disregarded?

Shell acknowledges "poverty and exclusion" (as the catalog repeatedly states) but denies its real, material, underpinnings—its broken slides, its dirty grounds, its poisoned and sickened bodies. In *hiding* actual life conditions, the catalog *reveals* the way in which a corporation seeks to signal its legitimacy (euphemized as "corporate social responsibility") in the face of massive suffering; a suffering that is factually denied at the same time that it is invoked.[9]

# 4

## The (Confused and Mistaken) Categories
## of the Dominated

Flammable can be quite deceptive to an outsider. If a stranger ventures into the neighborhood and starts talking to residents, they will immediately bring up toxic contamination as a topic. "There are kids here with six fingers," "Everybody here has cancer," and similar one-line expressions abound when the interlocutor is an outsider. In Flammable, people are quite used to strangers, mainly in the form of media reporters. Almost every other neighbor has talked to a journalist from one of the main TV channels or newspapers—some of them more than once. State officials, lawyers, and—less often—activists also pay frequent visits to the neighborhood and activate what amounts to a discursive repertoire. Flammable is known to outsiders as this contaminated place, residents seem to think, so let's give them what they are after: pollution talk. The discursive repertoire that the outsider encounters is a uniformed, coherent one: this is a contaminated place, contamination is bad for our health, authorities (or "my lawyer," in some cases) should (or will) do something about it. Things look quite different (neither homogenous nor definite) when neighbors talk among themselves in the course of everyday life. Although residents talk about their surroundings in many different ways, there are some recognizable themes in the stories they tell. In what follows, we scrutinize these stories because they provide us a window into neighbors' experiences of contamination and into their subjective, but not individual, categories of perception and evaluation regarding the sources, extent, and effects of industrial pollution.

Before we do so, one important caveat is in order: If we are to fully understand Flammable's toxic experience (or at least to approach the most adequate understanding we, together, are capable of) we also need to set all these stories in the context of lives characterized by many other pressing problems and highlight that periodically contamination recedes from consciousness (and thereby from open discussion).

The following pages might give the impression to the reader that all Flammable residents talk and care about is the surrounding dirt and pollution. Nothing can be further from the truth. Admittedly, residents are indeed worried (and, as we hope to demonstrate, confused) about the origins, extent and effects of air, soil, and water contamination. Contamination becomes the favored topic of conversation when journalists, lawyers, or state officials show up. But in the course of their daily lives, residents are also preoccupied with the same issues residents in most poverty enclaves are concerned about: how to make ends meets, growing crime, widespread use of drugs among youngsters, difficulties in finding a decently paid job (and, when both partners are lucky enough to have jobs, hassles about child-care arrangements), seemingly endless paperwork to obtain a pension, bureaucratic obstacles to accessing a welfare program, poor food quality at local state-funded soup kitchens, and the usual complications that abound in poor people's lives which are, to quote from Engels' (1993:139) classic study, "play-ball(s) to a thousand chances."

In the midst of these typical worries, contamination retreats from consciousness, and becomes, to a certain extent, routinized. Again, a visitor to the neighborhood would likely balk at the assertion that pollution has become normalized there because she would encounter people who are highly critical of their environment. Two years and a half of intensive fieldwork convinced us that most of the "pollution critical talk" (filled with disparaging comments about the surroundings and indictments against Shell and other compound companies) is, to a large extent, an artifact of outsiders' incursions. True, school students, when given a camera and the chance to portray the things they dislike about their neighborhood, gave us dozens of photos on (and disapproving comments about) the surrounding garbage and its disgusting smell (and, neighbors occasionally notice the noxious odors). But when they are playing in their backyards (see Photo 3.2), the dirt takes a background seat: they are playing and not analyzing themselves playing in the midst of garbage. We are not saying that they are used to garbage and contamination; we are simply stating that these are not subject of constant, sustained, scrutiny.

We cannot transcribe here the daily record of activities and conversations during our extended fieldwork—Débora's notes cover two thick notebooks. The reader will have to trust us on this: Flammable residents are not always talking about their risky and dangerous surroundings. It took us thirty months of traditional ethnographic fieldwork to figure out that the twin process of recession and normalization is permeated by the widespread confusion and uncertainty documented in the following pages. For outsiders, Flammable residents produce a clear-cut diagnostic of their plight; among themselves things get messier, less definite. Confusion and uncertainty, we will argue, are sociopolitical products that exacerbate residents' suffering.

## Denial and Displacement

Many people in the old part of Flammable, the one that sits right across from the compound, do not think of Shell as a contaminating source. Some of those who have worked inside the plant, including seventy-seven-year-old García, recount their own experiences in the plant to assure us that it is safe and that its premises are cleaner than we might think. When confronted with the lead study, García, and his wife, Irma, sixty-nine, assert that that is not an issue where they live; lead afflicts the shantytown dwellers. They are healthy; they have lived long lives, and so, their argument goes, nothing can be that bad in the environment. Others, like Silvia, are convinced that contamination is exclusively a shantytown problem.

Débora: People talk about all these contaminated children...what do you think about that?

García: I don't know, I don't know what contamination. They blame the coke plant, but the whole [industrial] process is a closed circuit, nothing is vented into the air. Years ago, the coal was all processed in the open...not even a single coal worker is alive. *That was unhealthy*...(original emphasis)

Irma: But not now...

García: No, not now. Listen, I worked there [in Shell] for thirty-eight years....They used to make gasoline with lead, but not anymore. I worked at the gasoline tanks, and I never got sick...When the Japanese came [reference to the study conducted by the Japanese Cooperation Agency, JICA] they didn't find anything. Shell is less contaminated than the city of Buenos Aires....

Débora: Do you know about the study [i.e., the lead testing]?

García: But that's [because] all the filth thrown by the Compañía Química [Chemical Company, inside the compound]. They threw acid. If you go to the houses that are on the other side and you dig a little you will find it's all full of filth, debris...

Irma: They brought garbage here...

Débora: Here, too?

García: No. Here we filled with soil...

Débora: So, how about the study?

García: I don't know...but don't forget that those kids are always barefoot.

| Irma: | The other day, three kids from the shantytown were swimming in a small lagoon that was formed after a rain . . . but they are not from here, they are from *el fondo* [the shantytown] . . . they might be contaminated. |
|---|---|
| García: | But not from the air, contamination is an issue there [in the shantytown]. |
| Irma: | In the landfills, in the landfills . . . |
| García: | If this were contaminated, imagine: she's been here since 1944, and I have lived here since 1950, we would be dead or sick but we were never sick because of contamination (*no tuvimos ninguna enfermedad de la contaminación*). . . . We've lived our whole lives here. I'm about to turn seventy-eight, and your [Débora's] grandfather is ninety. And we never got sick.[1] |

| Silvia: | [The kids who are contaminated] are all from there [the low-land, the shantytown]. None of the kids from here have any-thing. . . . Sometimes I wonder if I or my kids are contaminated. How long have you lived here? |
|---|---|
| Débora: | Since I was born . . . |
| Silvia: | My daughters are your same age. . . . It cannot be true that people who got here recently are contaminated, and they say it's because of *la empresa*. I don't know. I never felt sick. Sometimes I have bronchitis, or angina, but they never found anything in my blood. They [the children] get sick because all the garbage that they themselves collect. Not to say anything about the smell, it's pig-sty. Besides the smell that comes from factories. |

## Toxic Death

In the many formal interviews and informal conversations we have with neigh-bors, the issue of contamination comes out differently. Sometimes, residents bring up the subject spontaneously when speaking about how the neighbor-hood used to be ("this was all clean, now it's all contaminated") or when speaking about their daily routines ("With all the smell coming out from Tri Eco, I close my windows at night"). Other times, unless we make a specific inquiry about it (as with García and Irma), the issue remains submerged—evidence of the taken-for-granted or denied character of pollution. Ramiro does not wait for our questions. Early into our first conversation, he begins a long meditation—not always factually accurate—about the source, form, and effects of industrial pollution. It is interesting to note how he moves from inside the compound outward to Flammable's water, air, and soil. Note also that he brings up the issue of pollution without our prompting, and then he comes back to it even when talking about something different—evidence, for him, that "contamination is all over"—and links it, as do many other neighbors, to government corruption.

**Ramiro:** I used to work in construction. Most of the foundations of the tanks are made of concrete so that they can stand all the vibrations...

**Débora:** The vibrations?

**Ramiro:** There are machines, valves, because all the pipes carry gases. There are turbines, compressors.... There are machines that work with nuclear power. There's contamination inside, where there are the machines there's a lot of contamination, but nobody says anything here.... I'm talking about Shell, inside Shell. That coke plant should not be there. It came from Holland, and then [Governor] Duhalde and [Finance Minister] Cavallo and [Environmental Secretary] Alsogaray came and they received so much money [in bribes] and they shut up. Tri Eco is burning [i.e., incinerating] human corpses and that causes lung cancer. And who allows that to happen? The authorities, because they are all corrupt. Those chimneys should have filters, because they contaminate. When I go to sleep, sometimes I have to close the windows because of all the gases that come in.

Different from others who use their own health to deny (or question at least) the existence and extent of pollution, Ramiro remarks time and again on his own good health *despite* the surrounding contamination. He knows, intuitively at least, that different people respond differently to toxic assault: "See, fortunately I am a healthy person because, if not, I should be hyper-contaminated after forty-three years here." But not everybody is so lucky. He remembers his neighbor Virgilio, who had a farm nearby and who, he believes, was poisoned and died unexpectedly:

I used to ask Virgilio whether the water he used to drink in his farm was good or bad. "We've been here for one hundred years," he told me, "if it were contaminated, we would have died years ago." I had my suspicions, and I never drank from the water spigot in his farm. One day we had to carry the old man to the hospital, he had nausea, he had this white thing coming out of his mouth, as if it were some sort of intoxication. We took him to the hospital, and he never came back.

"Contamination is all over.... This has always been contaminated," Ramiro repeats oftentimes. To him, the lead contamination that became big news in the neighborhood three years ago is no surprise:

Listen, the air that we breathe has lead, the water the kids drink has lead. If they ever drank water from YPF, that water is contaminated. How can I explain it to you? Contamination is terrible.... Do you remember Pichón who used to work at Dapsa? Well, he had a car. Every time he left the car parked outside, it got corroded because of the acid that falls from the chimneys.... The land in which kids play is all contaminated, they play soccer there, day and night.... Contamination is latent, everywhere.... Lead is a fatal poison, in the long run it damages your heart.

Ramiro is so adamant about all the bad things in Flammable that we wonder out loud why he never left the neighborhood. Our question, formulated over the course of an extended conversation, did not produce the artificial response typical of survey questionnaires (Bourdieu 1999) but a reflection on all the things that slowly tied him to this (increasingly) polluted place. If properly read, we can detect how the gradual period of incubation of industrial pollution (in which farms slowly disappeared, streams got darker and dirtier, soils became filled with toxic garbage and debris) was lived mainly as a period of attachment to, of taking roots in, the neighborhood through work, family, and friendship networks:

**Débora:** Did you ever think about leaving the neighborhood because of all this contamination?

**Ramiro:** No. I came here for three months, and I'm still here. From 1962 to 2005, you do the math, I became fond of this place (*me encariñe con el lugar*).

**Débora:** Three months after which you planned to go elsewhere?

**Ramiro:** I thought it was going to be only a three-month period. After that I was going to leave so that the kids had better opportunities to study. And then, things began to work out, I made more friends here. The kids were able to take the bus to school. I had my little *quinta* [small farm] too. As I told you, I am from Laguna del Iberá. I was born and raised among animals, alligators, snakes... and

I came here and I found myself among the same little animals which reminded me of my place. And I had my quinta, and a job. Thank God I always had a job. And then . . . this was a small neighborhood. Four or five families, we all knew each other, we were like a family. We use to take care of each other. It was beautiful. I had nothing to complain about. I used to set the table out in the sidewalk and the neighbors came to eat. It was great. . . . I had plenty of work here . . . in Dapsa, in Shell. It was really peaceful (tranquilo) here; I left my clothes out and nobody would touch it. You could sleep with your doors open, and nothing happened, we all knew each other (eramos todos paisanos).

One day, Ramiro closed his doors because he heard a neighbor got robbed; another day he closed his windows because of the foul smell coming from the smokestacks; some other day he stopped tending his clothes outside because they got dark with the dirty air or because they got stolen. Who knows which reason came first? What we do know is that as things were slowly changing for the worse Ramiro was building up a family, enjoying his friends, and working, "always working." As the air, water, and soil got filthier, Ramiro was busy living his life: Flammable became "home." The process through which Ramiro and most of the old-timers in Flammable went through is crucial to understand how they think and feel about this (contaminated) place—not in the way an outsider would but in a way that is thoroughly embedded in history and the routine organization of daily life.

During these two years, we heard many neighbors, old and young, convey discomfort and uneasiness about Flammable's present state and future. Now that their place has become unfit for human habitation and their homes worthless, Flammable might occasionally feel that their neighborhood has become a trap ("Where else can I go?"), but it certainly did not seem one when residents were engaged in their busy daily lives.

## Suspicious Defiance

"Everything is contaminated here," says Liliana, who has been living in the area old-timers call the shantytown for twenty-three years and whose son suffers from chronic asthma. "Through a friend I found out that a group of people from the local university took soil samples . . . and it's all contaminated. On Sunday, a person from Channel 13 is going to come [to do a report]. He is going to go to each house to bring this to light (*para que esto se de a la luz*), so that people learn that the kids are contaminated and that the treatment that the municipal government was going to pay for never happened (*quedó todo en la nada*)."

She remembers the furor that the lead study caused:

> They [the government] said that there was going to be a treatment for the kids, that there was going to be a follow-up...that they were going to distribute aid...Reporters from *Punto Doc* [a popular TV program] came, and everybody got interested. Suddenly, tons of lawyers showed up...but in the end nothing happened....There are lots of kids with lead in their blood, and we don't really know, because in the future that might bring you trouble, some kids might even die.

Liliana sees the erratic labor of lawyers as matched only by the unpredictable work of state officials who "use us," who "make promises and never do anything," and who "tons of times have said that there was going to be a relocation but nothing happened." Now, "we are waiting for them to remove us...because this land has been sold." But "in the meantime they should do something because they are playing with the lives of grown-ups and of kids...the adults suffer from their bronchia, they also need a physical exam; those exams are expensive, and many people don't have the money. If I had the money, I would do [pay for] the study for my son, but I don't. We are here, waiting, with our arms crossed. It's not just a matter of relocation. The real issue is the children's health."

Liliana sees the companies in the compound as the source of contamination that is causing her son's asthma (the doctor at the health center told her that the asthma is caused "by the area where we live"). She also thinks that the companies are responsible for the lack of reliable electricity at her home, which she badly needs to make her son's nebulizer machine work. Like Ramiro and many others, she sees the issue of contamination as intricately related to governmental corruption. Like many others, she suspects that the companies "buy people off" to head off collective action. The coke plant, she said, was removed from Holland because "a lot of people who were getting sick got together [and struggled against it]...but here, there's a lot of disagreement, and there are many interests, and there's a lot of money, tons of money."

Despite the disappointment that came after all the media attention Flammable got after the lead study was publicized, Liliana still has hopes that the truth about lead poisoning will soon be known:

[The authorities] will find out through the media, and they will be ashamed.... They will realize that nothing happened, that the lead testing that was done years ago was useless... because we don't know whether their lead levels went up or down. We only know that something is wrong when a kid is sent to the emergency room because his lead levels were too high. That's not how things should be.... We are not animals.

Liliana is indeed defiant. She confidently asserts that contamination is, to borrow the words from Samantha [the local school ninth-grader], "killing us." And yet, despite her bold assertions, her daily experience is, like that of many others' here, dominated by suspicious about the actions of the compound companies, by uncertainties about the never-delivered, but always "imminent" actions of local authorities, and by a constant waiting for journalists to come and "show what's going on" and for lawyers to "do something about all this."

## On Not Knowing

Felisa is a beneficiary of the Plan Jefas y Jefes; in exchange for the monthly subsidy, she works part-time in the local health center—scheduling appointments for the several doctors that work there. Talking with her, we realize how practical knowledge about a dirty and contaminated place coexists with, on the one hand, discursive denial of the effects of contamination and, on the other hand, practices that may cause further poisoning and about which many residents remain blind.

Felisa knows, in practice, about the effects of dirt and contamination. Her son was recently bitten by one of the hundreds of rats that have thrived in the garbage that accumulates in nearby swamps and streets. Rashes and pimples (*granos*) are the most common causes of visits to the health center, she says. The doctors told her that they are caused by contamination. She also knows, in practice, how the state neglects the seriousness of the issue. As part of the center staff, she coordinated the lead screening and treatment for local children, which is now suspended. She attributes the suspension to local politics:

The treatment is about to start again; but I don't know when. The local government wants us to send the information [about lead-poisoned children] again. This is a new administration, and all we did before was with the other administration. And now everything has changed; the files got lost, and we have to start looking for the children again. And that's how it goes. If there's a new mayor, we will have to start all over again.

Despite all this practical knowledge, she does not seem to acknowledge that her own actions might be perpetuating the contamination of her own home. Since her backyard is still partly swamp, she and her husband routinely ask the trucks that bring garbage and debris to the nearby dump site to unload the contents in front of their home. They then take all the (possibly toxic) trash to the back. As attested to in the following interview excerpt, Felisa admits that the place might be contaminated. However, she remains uncertain about the real risk since her daughter is "not contaminated." As of herself, she cannot be sure because she cannot afford the costs of the medical examinations.

> **Felisa:** I don't really know [if pollution] is coming from the factories. They blame the coke plant. I had my daughter examined, and she was not contaminated. Doctors say it's because she goes to school outside the neighborhood, and because she is not constantly here, and because at night there is not so much pollution. I don't know, it's strange. She was born here, and she always lived here; so I don't really know what to say about the children who are contaminated with lead....
>
> **Débora:** Do you think that the air and the soil are contaminated?
>
> **Felisa:** Well, yes, it has to be contaminated. There are days in which you can't be here because of the smell. And the soil, too... plants live because they are plants. We are in a place where we cannot say there's no pollution. With so many factories, yes. We might be contaminated ourselves but since the adult population (*los grandes*) was not examined, we don't know. But the exam is expensive, and you can't do it by yourself. You can't afford it, *so you don't really know if you have something* (our emphasis).

### Understanding Uncertainty

With the black and white smoke coming out from the surrounding smoke-stacks, with the constant noise of alarms and heavy trucks, with the random odors of gas or other pungent substances, with the surrounding garbage and dirt swamplands, it is hard for anybody in Flammable to deny that the area is polluted. As we were repeatedly told (and experienced ourselves): "Sometimes you can't be outside, the odor stinks, your throat stings. It smells of gas. Even if we close our doors, it smells." And yet, when residents have to talk about the specifics of contamination, when they have to put a name to the sources, location, and contents of pollution things get murky. Doubts and mistakes also abound when neighbors speculate out loud about the deleterious health effects of pollution. In this section we further describe what we call "toxic uncertainty" and seek to explain its sources.

Flammable residents talk extensively about their environment. In analyzing our interviews and informal conversations, we found four manifestations of what we call "toxic uncertainty":

1. Misinformation—as when residents assume that lead contamination is clustered in the poorest section of the shantytown or when they assert that "lead is produced by the coal-processing plant."
2. Shifted responsibility—as when respondents argue that poor parenting is responsible for high levels of lead contamination.
3. Denial—as when residents actually challenge existing data showing that environmental pollution has reached toxic levels or when they use their own healthy bodies to deny serious contamination.
4. Blindness—as when neighbors ignore their own risk perpetuating land-filling practices.

Oil, for example, is said to contaminate water streams and to be harmless (the real problem being not the refinery but the storages of chemical substances); the refinery is believed to be completely safe or highly contaminating; the coke processing plant is seen as poisonous (so much so that it was "banned," according to many residents, from Holland) or innocuous (perceived as safe because it is "close"); Shell itself is seen as "the safest plant" or as the "worst of all," "giving presents around to cover contamination." With lead, however, discrepancies take a different form. Nobody denies that lead is harmful, but most displace it elsewhere: it is located not in the neighborhood but in the shantytown, it is stored not in their (or their children's) bodies but in those of the *villeros*. Although, as we described above, the JICA study showed no clear clustering or patterning of the lead cases, most people we talked to believe that lead is a real problem *in the shantytown* where kids play barefoot, where they do not wash their hands, where they swim in dirty waters. Rather than the environment itself, permissive mothers are, in this way of reasoning, those responsible for exposing children to lead.

Where does contamination come from? In neighbors' views, pollution is intricately related with government corruption—at every level of the government, from the mayor and the governor to the president. Plants (the Shell oil refinery, the coke processing facility, the hazardous incinerator, other refineries and chemical plants—past and present) contaminate because government officials allowed them to do so, and they allowed that to happened, so the generalized perception goes, because they were bribed. Rumors about the companies of the compound buying people off do not, however, restrict recipients to government officials. As we will see when we detail the "case of the wires," the common perception is that companies can (and routinely do) buy their way out of trouble. Ramiro nicely encapsulates the widespread conviction about the two-fold origin of pollution (from the smokestacks and from the government) in a single phrase when saying that "contamination comes from above" (*viene de arriba*).

How serious an effect does contamination have? As said, it is a matter of common knowledge that there is "something" in the air—there is less certainty or awareness about ground and soil pollution. But what people know (or say they know) is one thing, and how they interpret this information is quite another (Eden 2004; Vaughan 1990, 1998). On the one hand, one way of thinking and living pollution acknowledges its existence but denies its seriousness. And adults in Flammable use their own bodies to support that belief: after all, they "never had any health problem." On the other hand, another viewpoint expresses doubts concerning contamination's true effects because, so Flammable residents express, "they don't know yet." Countless of times we heard neighbors saying that they don't really know if they are "contaminated"—as if it were a black and white proposition, something that you have or you do not—because they have not yet been "tested."

Some people know contradictory things, they acknowledge the extent and severity of pollution but they also point the blaming fingers to the victims' own behavior as the true source of the contamination. Marga, the president of the local improvement association, illustrates what we think is a generalized uncertainty. As many others, Marga thinks "contamination is terrible. If you think about it and you start mulling over it, you want to leave this place right away." In talking about Flammable's past, Marga is convinced that the small farms disappeared because of all the industrial waste, "the soil was all contaminated, it stopped being useful." However, when speaking about the present, she expresses doubts about the true origin and form of lead contamination: "We should not put all the blame in those at the top. Parents are also responsible because they never cared to attend to their children and to see what could be done." She also says that she has many "doubts" regarding the degree of contamination: "I don't really know if I am polluted or not....I don't even know what the symptoms are." And yet she asserts, matter-of-factly, that the water streams are highly infected and that the shantytown population is deeply affected: "We are all responsible because we allowed these people [the shanty-town dwellers] to settle there, and we didn't provide good pipes for the water." As many others, she links pollution to government corruption: "The firms [in the compound] are not the sole wrongdoers. The municipal government did nothing to stop all those garbage dumps out there."

"So, you don't really know if you have something [implicitly referring to a disease related to contamination]," says Felisa. Many of the people in Flam-mable agree. Although the place is contaminated, and although they live in the place—surrounded by chemicals and garbage—they don't know that they themselves are contaminated. Or at least they don't know it yet. Residents have diverse interpretations regarding the spatial distribution of the contamination and its health effects. Pollution facts are, from the poisoned points of view, sometimes accurate and other times mistaken (as when lead contamination is thought of as clustered in the shantytown), unnoticed (as when their own risk-perpetuating land-filling practices are overlooked), or misinterpreted (as when they use their own health as a counterargument). How are we to understand and explain error, blindness, and confusion? How, in the midst of a slow-motion toxic disaster in which children have high levels of lead and where the air and water that residents breathe and drink are highly contami-nated, can Flammable dwellers allow themselves to doubt about (or, worse, deny) the "hard facts" of industrial pollution?

Although confusion and uncertainty are common human experiences, they rarely play a role in social-scientific analyses and ethnographic descriptions.[2] Puzzling, hesitant, contradictory words are suppressed from many ethno-graphic texts. As Wendy Wolford (2006:339) writes, "When we come across 'informants' who contradict themselves, or who can't explain their own moti-vations, we think of it as 'noise' and it gets edited out: nonsense, by definition, does not make sense." If doubts were to be "edited out" from our text, we would run the risk of completely misrepresenting the toxic lived experience of Flammable residents—pretty much along the lines of the media-driven dis-course that portrays the neighborhood as an "inferno" and its inhabitants as unidimensional beings, either "survivors" or "fighters" up in arms against the "big companies."

We would be running a similar risk of misrepresentation if we were not to attempt to *explain* the origins of the widespread confusion and uncertainty. An "ethnography of the particular" (Abu-Lughod 2000) should be complemented by socioscientific analysis of the causes of this specific way of experiencing contamination. Classic and current scholarship (Erikson 1976; Petryna 2002;

Eden 2004; Vaughan 2004) clearly shows that the sources of confusion and ignorance (about surrounding threats or risks) are not the individuals but the context. In our case, this context has slowly but steadily changed in the last seventy years and is plagued with inherent uncertainty and contradictory outside interventions. Since we already described the history of this place and the ways in which residents lived and perceived it, let us now dissect the multiplicity of incongruous, inconsistent, and many times, puzzling, interventions both material and discursive. We will see that the widespread uncertainty is, in part, the product of a labor of confusion performed, not necessarily intentionally and less so in a coordinated way, by a series of interconnected actors. We will also see that neighbors' insights into toxic assault and their defiance against its presumed culprits have affinities with some of these outside interventions.

## Uncertain Foundations

There are many confusing things about Flammable, and the source, extent, and effects of its contamination are hardly the only ones. To begin with, residents do not really know whether Flammable belongs under the jurisdiction of the state of Buenos Aires or of the general administration of ports (a branch of the federal state) which, in concrete terms, means that they don't know whether the state police or the coast guard is in charge of public safety in the area. This is a daily nuisance for neighbors because every time they file a complaint, the local police and the coast guard say the other one is in charge. When, during 2005, the phone wires were stolen (isolating further the oldtimers who live closer to the compound), neighbors went from the police precinct to the post of the coast guard vainly seeking someone who would claim authority to investigate the case. When there's a robbery, the same confusions over jurisdiction arise. When the garbage goes uncollected, neighbors don't know where to complain. A case in point is the May 2005 Dock Oil episode described in chapter 2 in which a local school student died after breaking into the abandoned building. For a couple of days, neighbors expressed their rage to the media reporters who covered the events over the fact that "nobody here takes charge." In this case, residents referred to the responsibility for answering the initial call and for investigating the case.

Flammable is, then, in the eyes of many residents, an authority-less land. State functionaries, on the other hand, acknowledge the jurisdictional jumble: one prominent municipal official we interviewed listed six government areas that have some sort of authority over Flammable: General Administration of Ports, Buenos Aires Department of Environmental Policy, Federal Department of Energy, Federal Department of Environment, Coast Guard, and the Municipality of Avellaneda (the official did not mention the different branches of the police that also intervene here).

Residents of Flammable are also doubtful about who is the real owner of the land and, consequently, about who can take the initiative if relocation is to happen. Plans for some kind of relocation (total or partial) had been on and off the drawing boards for several years. Rumors about imminent relocation, consequently, have been going around for at least two decades. ("Do you know how many times we were about to be relocated?" we were repeatedly asked.) The census that was being conducted while we were doing fieldwork, believed by residents to be part of a relocation plan, has been followed by no official action to that effect whatever—though rumors about residents "about to be displaced" have run rampant during the last two years.

In the more distant past, eradication was perceived as a threat, as a negative disruption of the life residents were living. As we will see in chapter 5, these days relocation is viewed in more ambiguous, somewhat more positive, terms given that neighbors imagine it will come together with a bulky monetary compensation. The shared view on relocation, as we will examine later, is now one of threat *and* anticipation.

### Fieldnotes (Javier), July 5, 2006

Laughing, imitating an old, toothless lady with a fake cane, Elsa (Débora's mom) says: "We are about to be relocated . . . soon, very soon . . . " We are having lunch at her house, and Elsa's imitation is her ironic response to yesterday's news published in *Clarín* [Argentina's main newspaper]. The news article reports that twelve companies (factories and storage facilities for mostly chemical plants) will be moved out of the compound. The report also says that 350 of the 700 families in Flammable will soon be relocated. The article reads: "It is not known yet which families are going to be relocated," and then cites municipal sources who told *Clarín* that seniority (i.e., years of living in the neighborhood) might be the criterion used to decide who will leave first. Elsa and her mother, Rosario, and Débora have read the news and, especially Rosario, were quite agitated: Would it be possible that after all these years they were going to be moved out? After all, their own family is among the oldest in Flammable.

> Today, before making my way to Flammable, I interviewed the secretary
> of public works of the Municipality of Avellaneda. He told me that there's
> nothing decided about the relocation—when I mentioned yesterday's
> news report, he explicitly asserted that he was not the "municipal source"
> cited by *Clarín*.
>
> Elsa, mocking herself twenty years from now "about to be relocated,"
> might be right after all. I have no way of knowing. Maybe relocation
> (of some or of everybody) will happen soon. What I do know is that the
> "threat" is a constant feature in their existence. Elsa, in one gesture,
> captures what many a resident feel: "We've always been about to be
> removed... and we will always be."

Stories about this or that firm (Petrobras, Shell, Central Dock Sud) purchas-
ing this or that portion of Flammable (the lowlands, the Danubio, the "four
blocks") to do this or that thing (to build, say, a parking lot, a garage, a storage
building) are part of everyday life in the neighborhood. Together with the confusion over the administrative jurisdiction to which the barrio belongs, these
doubts make life in Flammable uncertain.

People are also mystified about the compound itself and the adjacent industries. Nobody knows exactly how many companies are inside the compound's
premises nor what do these companies do—doubts that extend to Tri Eco, the
hazardous waste incinerator. In this last case, rumors range from the "burning of sick human cadavers" to the storage of "God knows what sorts of hospital products contaminated with AIDS." This confusion is understandable: not
even state officials were able to tell us how many companies are active inside
the compound. Reports oscillate between twenty-two (*Clarín*, Jan. 3, 2002),
thirty (*Telam*, Sept. 11, 2003; *La Nación*, March 30, 2004), forty (*Clarín*, Sept. 15,
2000), forty-two (*Clarín*, Sept. 19, 2001; *Página12*, June 23, 2002), forty-three
(*Clarín*, July 4, 2006) to fifty industrial plants and storage facilities (*Clarín*, Dec.
4, 2001). Regarding Tri Eco, officials admit that there are no real controls over
its activities.[3] The adjacent landfill is also an uncontrolled site—gas emissions,
typical of landfills, go unmonitored.

As we noted in the introduction, there is an intrinsic uncertainty about
toxic contamination (Edelstein 2004; Brown, Kroll-Smith, and Gunter 2000).
We cannot expect poor people, many of whom have not completed primary
or secondary education, to be highly informed about the concrete effects of
toxins, many of them unknown to physicians and scientists themselves. And
yet, what we observed is that in Flammable the inherent uncertainty of toxic

contamination is exacerbated by the actions and inactions of outside interventions, prominent among them those of the state.

> ### Fieldnotes (Débora), October 24, 2004
> Daniel, a neighbor who works for Shell, says that the Industrial
> Committee (an association of the compound companies) will soon talk
> to the owners of the homes in the neighborhood because Petrobras (the
> Brazilian oil company) does not want anybody in the neighborhood by
> 2005. According to Daniel, the Industrial Committee gave the money to
> the mayor to build the new houses.

> ### November 22, 2004
> Yesterday, as we were coming back from my aunt Herminia's house,
> the cab driver told me and my grandmother that all the people living in
> the shantytown will have to leave soon because a parking lot for a bus
> company is going to be built there (I never heard this version before!). He
> also said that all those living below the power lines "have to leave soon,
> because they [those living below the power lines] already got the money."
> And then adds: "Everybody should leave soon." My grandmother replies:
> "I've been living here for the last sixty years, and they always say the same
> thing."

> ### January 20, 2006
> Juan Carlos, my neighbor, tells me that he and some others went to talk
> to Prefectura about safety in the neighborhood.... Prefectura officials told
> him that they have no jurisdiction and that the group should send a letter
> to the Ministry of Interior.

## State (Mis)Interventions

Although outright official indifference toward the suffering of Flammable
residents clearly exists, understanding the various levels of government in
Argentina lends some nuance to the authorities' interrelations with the neighborhood. In the period immediately preceding our fieldwork, the city government put environmental contamination on the public agenda for the first
time. Let us elaborate on both what we think is a general thrust of government
neglect and on the details of the city action to problematize, for the first time,
the issue of environmental risk and vulnerability.

Residents' perceptions of Flammable as being under no one's authority are justified; since the building of the compound, no level of government
has done anything to regulate and control the activities that occur there. The
layout of the installations themselves betrays this total lack of regulation. As
the current undersecretary of environmental policy of Buenos Aires told us as
we were touring the compound's premises with him: "See the distribution of
tanks, gas tanks close to chemical tanks, pipes crisscrossing the area.... It's
basically the same thing that happened with urban space at large: it's all completely unregulated."

Companies inside the compound have basically been left to conduct their
own monitoring—with the consequences that neighbors now suffer. As
late as March 2004, the secretary of production and environmental policy of
Avellaneda publicly acknowledged that her office does not directly control
the plants inside the compound but relies on their self-reports. This lack of
oversight and control is certainly not unique to this location but is, according to former and current public officials we interviewed, typical throughout
Argentina. If the federal, the provincial, and the municipal governments were
unwilling or unable to control the activities within the compound, much less
so were they willing or able to monitor what went on in its adjacent land.[4]

Overall, the different levels of the state were unconcerned about industrial
pollution produced by the activities within the compound and its effects on the
people of Flammable. As far as we were able to reconstruct from drawing on
oral histories, published documents on the history of Dock Sud, and newspaper reports, environmental degradation and its pernicious health effects were
not even a public issue until fairly recently. Things began to change when a
progressive administration took charge of the municipal government in 1999,
and mainly when an inexperienced official—one still unaccustomed to being
politic—became the local secretary of the environment. With an academic
background in environmental sciences, this official, Máximo Lanzetta, made
"environmental risk and vulnerability" a public issue. In December 2000, at
the initiative of the municipal government, four levels of government—that of
the national administration, the province of Buenos Aires, the city of Buenos
Aires, and the municipality of Avellaneda—commissioned JICA to monitor the
air quality in the area surrounding the petrochemical compound and later to
conduct the epidemiological study cited in chapter 2 (and highly questioned
by Shell).

Both the "air" study and the epidemiological one generated intense community activity in Dock Sud and in Flammable. Meetings were organized by

the local municipality to explain the details of both studies and to solicit the cooperation of the local population. Noteworthy was the creation of a committee for environmental control—which lasted for about a year and a half and included representatives from both local and provincial governments, community associations, and compound plants.[5]

While these studies were being conducted and community meetings proliferated, several local schools in Dock Sud were evacuated because of reports of "toxic leaks," presumably coming from the nearby compound. These episodes, together with the massive publicity received by the "Japanese study" (as many neighbors still call it) and with the public speeches of both the mayor of Avellaneda and his young secretary of environment calling for better controls of the compounds activities and emissions had a stirring effect on the local population (see, e.g., La Prensa Nov. 8, 2001).[6] In November 2001, approximately two hundred Dock Sud residents (including some from Flammable) erected a roadblock at the entrance to the compound, effectively stopping the circulation of hundreds of trucks for a few hours. It was the first roadblock (piquete) organized to draw attention to the area's contamination. One protester in the roadblock summarized the piquete's demand this way (encapsulating state's indifference and anticipating, unknowingly, things to come): "We are always suffering the consequences of toxic leaks, and nobody does anything. They come, they take a look, they listen to us, and they leave" (Diario Popular, Nov. 8, 2001). It would be hard find a better expression of the past and present relationship between Flammable residents and the state.

This protest generated a revealing polemic among government officials: the mayor of Avellaneda accused the government of Buenos Aires of "protecting and defending the private firms of the compound, when it should be protecting the health of the neighbors of Dock Sud" (Diario Popular, Nov. 10, 2001). Mayor Laborde demanded the transfer of the power and the resources to control the compound activities. Buenos Aires government officials swiftly replied that "the municipality already has jurisdiction over the compound... this polemic makes no sense." The mayor, in turn, said candidly, "On the one hand there are the companies that contaminate and on the other is the government of Buenos Aires that is not controlling them as it should." At the center of the polemic were the affected neighbors ("as if we were in a tennis match," said the president of Dock Sud's improvement association; Diario Popular, Nov. 10, 2001). We would not be focusing attention in this internal debate among officials if not for the fact that we think it illustrates the way in which the problem of industrial pollution and its real-life consequences usually are treated by federal and provincial authorities: *as a problem whose solution is always someone else's responsibility.* A reproach made by a state official from the province of Buenos Aires to the local secretary of environment when the latter publicized the results of the JICA report summarizes the federal and provincial state's views of the problem: "Since you [referring to the official who was broadcasting the JICA report to national media] created the problem, you have to solve it." As the former local secretary of environment told us: "This is how officials see the issue of contamination, as a problem that some of us create for them." Lanzetta aptly refers to the JICA report as an "Exocet": a missile capable of inflicting a lot of damage to government officials.

Local government activity regarding industrial pollution reached its peak in August 2003 with the release of the second JICA report. Following the publication of the epidemiological study that showed the presence of lead and other toxic chemicals in the blood of children of Flammable, the mayor asked the local penal courts to find out where the "probably carcinogenic emissions" were coming from. That was on August 9, 2003, and the courts have not produced any indictment as of today. A month later, the president of Argentina and the governor of the province of Buenos Aires signed an agreement to relocate the petrochemical compound. In a public meeting celebrated in one of the local schools that, only two years earlier, had to be evacuated because of a toxic leak, President Néstor Kirchner said:

> We want companies to come [to Argentina] to produce, but we are tired of them coming at any cost. . . . These companies generated a lamentable environmental situation. . . . The environment is part of our riches and part and parcel of our quality of life. [The compound] is an affront to the dignity of all Argentines. (*Telam*, Sept. 11, 2003)

Neither local officials nor Shell personnel took the relocation agreement or the public announcement that followed seriously. Government officials and Shell personnel who are usually on opposite sides of the debate noted that no legal papers had been signed. When we interviewed the current secretary of environment of Avellaneda, she said that the agreement for the compound's relocation was an "optical illusion." And events seem to have proved them right. Aside from the noncompulsory lead screening for the children, nothing has been done to address the problem of environmental contamination and massive poisoning head-on, even despite a federal Supreme Court decision that ordered the different government branches to urgently address pollution in Argentina, citing, among other examples, the case of Flammable (see chapter 5). In point of fact, addressing toxic suffering has never been at the top of anybody's policy agenda in the country.

How can residents *not* be confused, puzzled, and sometimes angered if officials, presumably in charge of their well-being, send such a barrage of (contradictory, confused, and sometimes defiant) messages? On the one hand, state officials raise the issue of contamination, publicly denounce the companies of the compound for its health-threatening emissions, push for a thorough study of the extent and effects (though not of the sources) of industrial pollution, and (in the words of none other than the president himself) promise the relocation of the compound (as late as July 2006, some municipal officials were openly admonishing that removal of all the companies was the only "real solution").[7] On the other hand, officials randomly show up in Flammable talking about relocation of the neighborhood (not the compound). They then disappear without leaving traces of this or that relocation plan—which explains the manifold rumors regarding future living arrangements for Flammable residents, from a housing project in far away suburbs to individual duplexes in nearby Dock Sud. State officials, furthermore, push for a thorough lead-screening program that is then suspended and, later, restarted. In this way, the state's "averted gaze" (represented in the words and deeds of high and low level officials) feeds uncertainty and confusion "by its implacable opacity, its refusal to comprehend, and its inability to act responsively to the human suffering that presents itself" (Scheper-Hughes 1992:294). If the state is *simultaneously* confused, neglectful, and bold, why should we expect otherwise from sick and weak neighbors?

## Doctors' Misunderstandings

The study of illness meanings is not only about one particular individual's experience; it is also very much about social networks, social situations, and different forms of social reality. Illness meanings are shared and negotiated. They are an integral dimension of lives lived together.... Illness is deeply embedded in the social world, and consequently it is inseparable from the structures and processes that constitute that world. For the practitioner, as for the anthropologist, an inquiry into the meanings of illness is a journey into relationships.

Arthur Kleinman, *The Illness Narratives: Suffering, Healing, and the Human Condition*

Several times, in the course of formal interviews or informal talks, Flammable residents told us that the local doctors advise them that, if they and their children are to be cured, they have to move out of Flammable. Other times, residents report the confused and confusing silence of doctors concerning their complaints or their recourse to an "aspirin prescription"—which residents know full well does nothing. Some of them even suspect that because the doctors are paid by Shell, they have bought into quietude—whereas the truth is that although the local center was built and equipped with Shell money, doctors are paid by the local state.

Twice during the course of our fieldwork, we had extensive interviews with physicians at the local health center. Their responses to our queries regarding the population's precarious health and its connection to environmental contamination are, in more than one way, puzzling. Denial is mixed with, on the one hand, utter ignorance regarding the *documented* links between poison and individual health and, on the other hand, with their own suspicions about, in a doctor's own words, "something strange going on here."

During our first visit (July 2004), a team of three doctors and a nurse talk to us about the common health problems of the population in Flammable. Relying on their experience in other poor areas, all agree that the pathologies affecting Flammable residents are no different from those seen in other impoverished enclaves. In a diagnosis that separates something that usually comes together (i.e., poverty and environmental degradation), one doctor matter-of-factly tells us that illnesses in Flammable are the result of poverty, not of contamination. Respiratory diseases, they say, are caused not by pollution but by problems that poverty brings, such as overcrowding. When we query them about the uncommon presence of a health center with a twenty-four-hour emergency service, an operating ambulance, and seven working doctors on site, their common reply further accentuates our doubts: Well, yes, it's rare . . . nothing is what it appears to be in Flammable," one says.

### Fieldnotes (Débora), July 25, 2005

LOCAL MYSTERIES. The doctors tell us that this health center might be losing money because few people attend, and it is very well equipped when compared to other health centers. We interviewed the doctors in a room that had a map of the neighborhood hanging from a wall. The map was made by a social worker who intended to keep a record of the most common sicknesses in the neighborhood. The social worker was fired, and she took all the data with her. The doctors were surprised. So were we.

This morning I spoke with Felisa (the center's nurse). She was going to help me to map the lead cases (to see if there's a clustering in some parts of the neighborhood). But the director of the health center [a doctor himself, paid by the city government] told her not to help me. He told Felisa that lead is "their" issue and that we should not try to further expose the families. I told Felisa that I already interviewed the mothers of lead-poisoned kids and that they had no problem whatsoever. I told Felisa that I could speak with the director but she told me not to do so. I draw the map myself without their help.

A year later (July 2005), we interview a pediatrician and a clinician who work mornings at the health center. They also deny the existence of sicknesses that are exclusive to Flammable. The anemia and allergies they treat here are quite common in other poor areas: "What you see here is the same thing you treat in [poverty-ridden] Solano." When quizzed specifically about the probable effects of pollution they (in the individualizing logic typical among doctors) tell us that in order to fully know about the issue, case-by-case studies have to be conducted. But, somehow contradictorily, they add that the local population has to be relocated because "this area is inhabitable" (incidentally, one of the JICA I air quality monitors was located at the health center and registered higher than normal concentrations of benzene there). They also report two recent cases that in a way cast doubt on their own judgments regarding the effects of contamination: "A while ago, two women became blind. That might be because of contamination."

These two doctors do not know much about the JICA study on lead and think (wrongly) that lead affects only the children of adults who work with lead (persons who work with car batteries, for example). There are no contamination-related diseases here, they repeat several times. And yet, throughout our talk it becomes apparent that they have very little training in the detection and diagnosis of these kinds of diseases. In seven years of study at the school of medicine, they took only one class on environmental health. One of them tried to dispel her own never fully articulated uncertainties about the place by having herself tested (for lead, chrome, and toluene). As if to reinforce the negative results of these tests, both doctors add that a former physician left the center because she claimed she was contaminated with toluene. (Sandra, whose story we summarized in the opening of this book, still thinks the doctor left because of lead poisoning.) Apparently this physician was tested again at her new workplace, and her levels of toluene where higher. So, they deduce, the problem can't be with Flammable.

Doctors at the local health center are not alone in this ignorance mixed with suspicions. The associate director of the main hospital of Avellaneda (and one of the largest in Buenos Aires) told the Federal Ombusdman office that his hospital did not have the ability "to identify the toxic substances or to conduct studies" on contamination-related illnesses. In his interview with the Federal Ombudsman team, this high-level functionary said he knew about the JICA study but ignored its results. The Ombudsman report also points out that the hospital's executive director might have had "ties" with the companies of the petrochemical compound (Defensoría del Pueblo de la Nación Argentina, 2003:249). Officials from the Federal Ombudsman office found the same lack of factual knowledge among the physicians of the Hospital Ana Goitía (specializing in pregnancies, births, and neonatology) and of the Hospital Cosme Argerich (both hospitals serve the population of Flammable).

Three interrelated elements emerge from the above. They are all crucial to understanding Flammable residents' experiences of pollution. First, the most obvious one: doctors are quite ignorant about environmental illnesses. Second, local health center doctors have a medical orientation that, according to a distinction that Kleinman makes, focuses exclusively on "disease" and neglects "illness," the human experience of symptoms and suffering, the ways in which individual's network of relatives, friends, and neighbors "perceive, live with, and respond to symptoms and disability" (1988:3). To residents such as Sandra, Felisa, Daniel, Ramiro, or, as we will see below, Verónica, the uncertainty about present toxic contamination and its future effects is a source of real suffering. That suffering, however, has no place in physician's perspectives.

Third, and related, in physicians' (and, we should add, in Shell's) views, medical or scientific facts suppress (or, better, delegitimize) the widespread anxiety of Flammable residents, men and women alike, concerning pernicious health effects of toxins. It seems ironic, even cruel, that Flammable residents, after having offered their children to detailed physical and psychological examination for the JICA II study and afterward during the irregular lead-screening program coordinated by the local government, are now being told that their fears and anxieties about their own health and that of their children are unfounded. A caveat, however, is in order. Although physicians say there are not specific health pathologies in Flammable, they have also advised their patients—according to residents—to move out of Flammable because their (or their children's) sickness might be related to where they live. We have no way of telling whether doctors actually conveyed this to their patients; what is important is what residents sometimes *hear* from the doctors they (usually, though not always) trust. The contradictions of physicians' deeds and words and the tensions between their public discourse and individual experiences are further sources of confusion. How can local residents *not* be mystified if even local doctors are confused and/or wrong about the sources of suffering in Flammable? How can puzzlement and mistake *not* be perpetuated amid a barrage of contradictory discourses? How can residents *not* be suspicious about possible ties between doctors and the compound that might be suppressing knowledge about the latter's pernicious health effects when even doctors themselves have these reservations?[8]

## The Media

### Fieldnotes (Javier), August 17, 2004

At approximately 3 P.M., a whole crew from Channel 13 arrived at Eugenio's house (a few years ago, he had been the vice president of the local improvement association and worked for the former undersecretary of environmental policy at the local municipality). Eugenio and Marga (current president of the improvement association) called upon neighbors to "come and tell the reporters what's going on." Several mothers of lead-poisoned children were among the small crowd of twenty or so. It was certainly strange to see Otero (a famous anchorman on national TV) in person here, wearing a tie and suit and with his face full of makeup. One cameraman, the executive producer of the news program, four municipal officials (who work at the ombudsman office and oppose the current mayor), and a physician from the Argerich Hospital came in two vehicles and parked right in front of Eugenio's across from a big swampland. They came, so a member of the crew tells me, to "report on the effects of contamination on the local population." The mothers of leaded children came with the hope of obtaining some help (medicine and/or treatment for their sons and daughters). Otero interviewed Marga, who complained bitterly about contamination coming from the compound, and to Alejandra, who spoke softly, her hand covering her missing teeth for the camera, about her lead-poisoned child. Otero then proceeded to interview the doctor who came with them. With the help of Eugenio, Otero and the doctor moved to the border of the swampland. With the dirty and stagnant waters as the chosen background, the doctor, in an impeccable white uniform, spoke about the highly dangerous toxins in the air of Flammable and the devastating health effects of pollution. The episode lasted for approximately twenty-five minutes and was observed by personnel of the Prefectura Naval, who stood a block or so from the crowd and who, according to one neighbor, were there to "control." The doctor did not talk to the neighbors. The whole thing looked bizarre.

At the time Javier wrote this entry, he did not know the extent to which neighbors were used to the presence of media reporters. Soon, however, he realized that TV and print reporters were frequently in Flammable to talk about one subject: pollution. Neighbors' views of media reporters are ambiguous. One the one hand, residents are very aware of the fact that the more the reporters come into the neighborhood, the higher their chances of being heard and of the state responding to their plight. As Liliana puts it, the authorities "will find out through the media, and they will be ashamed . . . they will realize that nothing happened, that the lead testing that was done years ago was useless." As in many other territories of urban relegation, the media are seen as one of the few channels through which people can make themselves heard. Residents have an intuitive sense that their fence-line lives are newsworthy, and they volunteer their time when reporters and news photographers show up.

However, Flammable residents are also annoyed at what they see as the media "uses" of their plight. Many times during the course of our fieldwork we heard expressions that convey this irritation with reporters who come to the neighborhood and promise help in exchange for "our story" and then vanish. "This guy from *PuntoDoc* told us that he was going to send us clothes and stuff and never showed up again," one resident said.

But the media interventions are a source of confusion for Flammable residents not because reporters come and go and purportedly make use of the neighbors' suffering. Media baffle residents because they randomly come into the neighborhood, focus on the most extreme aspect of life here, and then broadcast the news in the authoritative language of journalism (with the help of the occasional experts) emphasizing how improbable life is in Flammable. Neighbors say that the media focus on "bombs" only to disappear a couple of days after the explosion (producing one-line attention-seeking headlines such as "half of the children are contaminated," "the compound causes cancer," or things of that like). Reporters seem oblivious to what one basic truth: residents of Flammable are not only producers of stories for the media, they also consume these reports (mainly those broadcast on TV). Their stories move out from the neighborhood to the TV and they come back as one-sided, sensationalized scripts of dreadful lives directed at the larger public's consumption. If the media unanimously tell them their life is an impossible one we wonder:

How can they *not* be puzzled? If reporters come to the neighborhood, promise help in exchange for a "story," and then disappear without trace until they reappear on the TV screen, how can residents *not* be confused?

### *Fieldnotes (Débora), April 5–19, 2005*

I ran into Karina Olmos today; her kid is lead-poisoned. She showed me all the pimples and rashes on her arms. . . . She was very angry about *PuntoDoc* (the TV program) and Channel 13 because they promised her clothes, a house, and some other things and never showed up. . . . When days later I bumped into her at the local school, she told me that her youngest kid was having some health problems, and that the oldest one had some sort of allergy, her hands were all swollen. She didn't know what to think about it.

## Words of Power

Residents' eyes are neither fully closed nor wide open to their polluted surroundings. Their views are much more varied. They range from what Paul Willis (1977) would call "partial penetrations"—insights into the causes (varying from corporate greed to government corruption) and effects (extending from their health to that of their offspring) of industrial pollution—to a much more widespread uncertainty. School students, for example, are quite certain (though, in some cases, factually equivocal) about the sources of contamination. Their adamant points of view come, we believe, from some of their teachers' insistence on contamination as a widespread problem in the neighborhood. Many teachers at the local school also believe that Shell, despite the "social promotion plans" with which it showers the neighborhood, and the other compound companies are responsible for the barrio's toxic suffering; these beliefs also resonate in their students' voices. But once we step outside of the school, perceptions cease to be uniform; doubt prevails. This chapter focused on the form this uncertainty takes and its endogenous and exogenous origins.

Confusion and doubt are indeed socially constructed. But the construction of mystification is hardly a cooperative creation. What physicians have to say about health in the neighborhood (and what they silence) carries a different weight than, say, what Karina Olmos has to say. What the president or other state officials affirm, do, or avoid doing matter more than what Don Nicanor asserts or does. What Shell or, as we will see in the next chapter, some other compound company says (and denies) and does (and avoids doing) are much more consequential than what even the most defiant or angriest of neighbors can accomplish. Opinions and interventions are, we know, endowed with different power (Williams 1977; Thompson 1984; Bourdieu 1991; Perrow 1999). Some actors have a bigger influence on the way Flammable's toxic reality is constructed and perceived. In echoing these dominant and contradictory practical and discursive interventions, residents' narratives show us that the culture of toxic uncertainty is, indeed, a complex web of meanings and shared understandings. Residents' voices also show us that this culture of toxic uncertainty is molded by displays of (material and discursive) power. We will come back to a more formalized view of different sources of confusion and uncertainty in chapter 7, but before we do so we would like to focus attention on the effects that generalized confusion and uncertainty have on residents' hearts and minds and on their recursive relationship with collective action and inaction.

Back in 1999, residents jointly protested against Central Dock Sud's installation of a high-voltage wire close to (in some cases on top of) their homes. This ultimately failed attempt at collective action, the lessons residents learned from it, and the ongoing legal battle over the "case of the wires" constitute the subject of the next chapter.

# 5

## Exposed Waiting

Waiting is one of the privileged ways of experiencing the effect
of power. . . . Waiting implies submission.
Pierre Bourdieu, *Pascalian Meditations*

In one of the many versions of the Greek myth that have been handed to us, early in life Tiresias surprises Athena while she is taking a bath. As punishment for having seen her naked, Zeus's daughter blinds young Tiresias but comforts him with the gift of seercraft. As Alfred Schutz reminds us in his inspiring essay "Tiresias, or Our Knowledge of Future Events," Tiresias has the knowledge of things to come but in the present time our mythical seer can neither see what actually happens nor bring things about or prevent them. "He remains," Schutz writes, "an impotent onlooker of the future" (1964:277).

The myth of Tiresias serves Alfred Schutz as a springboard to examine the ways in which the commonsense thinking of ordinary men and women "anticipates things to come" (281), and, more generally, to distinguish between the realm of the social world that is beyond human control and that upon which individuals can act—between "events that will occur without our interference and those to be brought about by our actions" (291).

Human beings resemble Tiresias, Schutz says, insofar as a large sector of the world in which they live escapes their control. Our very existence depends on events we neither effect nor affect, but we are, like the mythical seer, "mere unconcerned onlooker[s] of the future [we] envision" (282); unlike Tiresias, however, our anticipations concerning these events are "governed by hopes and fears" (292). In the world of future events that we assume can be influenced by human conduct, men and women are the exact opposite of Tiresias: "We consider ourselves the makers of these events" (292). In contemporary socio-anthropological language, women and men think of themselves as *agents* and act accordingly. An agent's world is an intention-full realm, a world of "projects": visualizations of states of affairs to be brought about by our future action (Emirbayer and Mische 1998).

Schutz's reading of the myth of Tiresias points to a theme that has been extensively discussed in classical and contemporary social theory and empirical research, namely the manifold ways in which human beings in their life-worlds think and feel about (and act on) *time* (Sorokin and Merton 1937; Roth 1963; Geertz 1973; Zerubavel 1979; Giddens 1986; Flaherty 1999). In the first of Schutz's worlds, individuals, whether afraid or hopeful, have to *endure* time. "Like the spectator at the theater," the individual is a sheer observer "of what is going to happen" (292). In the realm of human action, on the contrary, agents can *act* (or *project*) on a time that they perceive as malleable.

The myth of Tiresias also draws attention (in ways that Schutz's focus on the universal character of time perception prevents us from fully exploring) to a connection between *time* and *power*. Time, for example, has been analyzed as a crucial dimension in the workings of gift exchanges (Bourdieu 1977) and in the operation of patronage networks (Scott and Kerkvliet 1977; Auyero 2001). In both these cases, the objective truth of these exchanges needs to be *misrecognized* so that the exchanges can function smoothly (Bourdieu 1998; Ortner 2006). Time is responsible for the veiling.

Temporality, these analyses reveal, is manipulable. It can be the object of a "continual process of bargaining," as Julius Roth (1963) shows in his insightful ethnography of the ways in which patients and doctors jointly structure the passage of time in a sanatorium for tubercular patients; the object of constant onslaught, as Paul Willis (1977) illustrates in his dissection of the ways in which students fight over the school's timetable; or the medium through which discipline is imposed and negotiated, as E. P. Thompson (1994) demonstrates in his classic analysis of the changes in the inward notations of time at the early stages of industrial capitalism. Collective time senses are deeply intertwined with the workings of (and resistance to) social domination. Time, these works expose, is the locus of conflict but also, just as important, of acquiescence.

One of the many things that surprised us during our fieldwork in Flammable was that, almost always, expressions about present-day contamination and its suspected (or denied) health effects came hand in hand with statements regarding events that would happen in the imminent future. If not for the fact that this collapse of present and future made the coding of interviews and fieldnotes a daunting task, we might not have noticed the fascinating analytical challenge in front of us. In our interviews and informal conversations, we noticed that oftentimes statements that expressed doubts and confusions about what was currently going on merged with assertions that communicated confidence about the near future.

The ways in which residents of Flammable think and feel about (and cope with) pollution are, we note during our fieldwork, deeply entangled with their perceptions of the future. An ethnographic account of the lived experiences of contamination should thus be, at the same time and by logical necessity, a tempography—a thick description of the sociotemporal order that prevails among residents.[1]

Beliefs about pollution are constructed in time. Time, we will argue in this chapter, gives experiences of contamination its form and meaning—so much so that it would be impossible to describe and explain the generalized uncertainty that dominates Flammable lives without at the same time dissecting perceptions of time, and in particular, residents' hopeful/fearful waiting.

This chapter will not only show that perceptions of toxicity are rooted in beliefs about the future; we will also demonstrate that residents understand this future as something beyond their control. Much like every other human being in her "wide-awake reality," Flammable residents are, as Schutz would argue, highly involved in what they anticipate; their expectations, furthermore, are shared, collective, socialized. One could certainly interpret their (sometimes illusory) expectations as ways (not necessarily conscious) in which residents actively seek to structure uncertainty. And yet, with respect to their contaminated environment, Flammable residents also resemble Tiresias: they experience contamination as something that escapes their control and as something toward which the dominant stance is that of waiting for the powerful to decide over their lives. Like Tiresias, Flammable residents are powerless witnesses of the actions and words (or lack thereof) taken or said elsewhere. Let us present our argument through a detailed reconstruction of Verónica's predicament.

### Verónica's Afflicted Hopes

| | |
|---|---|
| Verónica: | We are going to move to Tucumán. |
| Débora: | To live there? |
| Verónica: | Yes. To live there. It's nice there. It's different. Did you see what happened yesterday? Josefina got robbed. And they [the thieves] are kids from the neighborhood, kids who you and I know, kids that we say "hi" to every day.... |
| Luis [her husband]: | I don't know if we are going to move to Tucumán. It's hard to get a job there... |
| Verónica: | *But we are going to have money, Luis!* |

The dialogue takes place on March 2005. The day before, an old-time neighbor's house was burglarized. Verónica wants to move out of Flammable not only because of its increasing violence but because of its "horrible" environment, "all filled with garbage and rats…all contaminated." Luis has doubts about the likelihood of Verónica's plans. He knows it will not be easy to find a job in the northern province of Tucumán. Verónica believes that work will not be their primary concern in their future destination: She expects to receive a huge sum of money from the courts sometime soon. She and seventeen other neighbors are suing the transnational electrical company Central Dock Sud. They are demanding thousands of dollars in compensation for the damages caused by the installation of a high-voltage wire line that runs on top of their precarious shacks (see Photo 5.1). The wires, Verónica and her brother Daniel believe, "cause us a lot of health problems."

Verónica is twenty-seven years old but, as many of her young neighbors, looks much older. Every time we see her, she looks exhausted. She is another beneficiary of the Plan Jefas y Jefes. Luis, her husband, works as a stevedore in the nearby port of Buenos Aires. Verónica tells us that "he works for a week, and then he can't find a job for a month, he works for three days, and he is out

**Photo 5.1** "The trucks, the wires, and the houses." (Photo taken by Javier Auyero)

of work for five days.... He works in the ships, always part time (*una changa*), never effective, never full time. Maybe he works for an entire month and then he is out of a job for the next five months."

Verónica has three children: Alexis, seven years old; Gonzalo, four; and Nara, two. Verónica's twenty-three-year-old brother, Daniel, lives in a small room on the back of their house. He is a source of constant concern for Verónica because he has been involved in petty crime for the past two years. Daniel is not a very successful criminal. On June 2004, while he was trying to steal some iron bars from a nearby storage facility, a private security guard fired at him with a home-made pistol that filled his head and body with pellets. "See, touch my head," he tells us, "they [the pellets] are still here. They make me very nervous." A year later, he was wearing a cast on his left leg: another failed attempt to steal from a local warehouse ended with a broken leg that required surgery. Verónica was not able to register Daniel for the Plan Jefas y Jefes. Daniel's explanation is that "there are a lot of crooks there, and you have to befriend one of the coordinators, who take away part of your benefit." When Daniel is not around, Verónica tells us that she tries to buy clothes and other necessities for him "to keep him away from la joda (crime)."

Verónica keeps a close eye on her brother, but her main source of worry is Gonzalo, who was diagnosed with a spinal defect called Arnold Chiari malformation at birth.[2] Gonzalo is undernourished and suffers from celiac disease. He also has, Verónica tells us, "hearing problems, half of his face has been paralyzed since he was born, he has torticollis, and he has six fingers on his hand...Gonzalo, show your hand to him." Verónica worries about the high-voltage wires; though they did not cause Gonzalo's birth defects—they were installed after he was born—they might exacerbate his condition. "I was living here while pregnant with Nara and thank God she is healthy. I don't know if Gonzalo got this because of the contamination.... The doctors tell me I have to move out from here, because as his illness gets worse, things are going to become more complicated for him if we stay here. Those wires release some sort of acid that is awful.... But I don't have money to move out of here." Like Sandra Martinez (described in the opening story of this book), Verónica is always short of money, and so she oftentimes cannot pay for medication for Gonzalo's random convulsions. "Yesterday we had to run to the hospital because we were out of medicine," she says. During the past months, efforts to raise money for Gonzalo have occupied most of her time. She went to the Catholic Church charity association (Caritas) for aid but says she received nothing. She also went to the local municipality "to speak to the wife of the mayor. The secretary told me that they couldn't be blamed for my son's disease. I wanted to kill her, but I was with Gonzalo. And he gets very nervous if he sees me angry, and he starts with convulsions. So I left." She also contacted Mr. Sieppe, Shell's PR director, and asked him for wood panels to build a special room for Gonzalo. The request was denied. Neighbors see Verónica as a sufferer but also as a fighter; she "never gives up," said María, who lives in the old section of Flammable. "The things she does for that kid—she's admirable."

Verónica has applied for municipal money to improve Gonzalo's room a multitude of times over the past four years. In the dialogue that follows we see how her frustrations with government inaction meet and mesh with her disgust with the neighborhood and with her fears that environmental toxins are harming her and her loved ones. Her life is, like many other lives in Flammable, a frustrated waiting time: waiting for the local welfare agents to deliver, waiting for hospitals to provide medicine. As we will later see, her life is also about a hopeful waiting for the lawyers to come, for the physicians to conduct the physical examination that will prove the harmful effects of the high-voltage wires, and for the judge to rule in their favor. Verónica and her family will then, she hopefully expects, be able to move out of Flammable.

> **Débora:** So, did a social worker from the municipality ever come here to see you?
>
> **Verónica:** Yes. A social worker came. She says they will bring the stuff [referring to material to build an addition]. Then she says they will be here the day after tomorrow. Y nunca más ["they never showed up again"]. The other day I went to the hospital, and I left at 1 P.M. I talked to the nutritionist and told her that Gonzalo had low weight. She said that Gonzalo needed this and that. She told me that they were going to send the stuff [referring to food and medicine] the next day. I'm still waiting...
>
> **Débora:** And nothing happened?
>
> **Verónica:** They never showed up. I am not asking for money, I am not asking for a new house. I'm only asking for wood to build a new room for him. Because the one he has now...well, you know, even if I clean it all the time, when the lagoon [water level of the swamp] goes up, there're a lot of rats [her backyard extends into a swampland]. And even if I spread poison, the rats are still around. There are rats this big. Those are not mice, those are rats! If you put poison or traps, they are still around.... They are

huge. And if they bite one of the little guys or if they touch something in your kitchen.... I never leave food on the table because
you never know. I'm always cleaning, I put bleach on the chairs,
the tables. I ruined these chairs with so much bleach.

The several times we visited Verónica, she was always cleaning. She is very
concerned about the garbage that accumulates in the neighborhood. "We
need to ask for a container here.... This cannot keep going, there's garbage
all over the place."[3]

She, like the youngsters in the local school, sees herself as living in the
midst of garbage, rodents, and contamination. Regarding the latter, she, like
many of her neighbors, is suspicious about the effects. Could contamination,
she wonders out loud, be responsible for her child's birth defects?[4] She is also
uncertain (and sometimes mistaken) about its *origins* ("It's not Shell alone.
It must be Tri Eco, too, where they burned all the dirt from hospitals. They
burned dead bodies there. People who are sick in the hospitals, they cut their
legs off and they burn them here. Tri Eco burns the waste of hospitals, from
AIDS, from tuberculosis, for syphilis, all that dirt is being burned by Tri Eco.
We are breathing all the refuse from the human body") and its *extent* ("The
water here is good. Well, that's what we say, we feel it's normal, but it'd be
good to have it tested. It's not the same water you drink elsewhere, it's kind of
strange.... They say the soil is contaminated. But my kids were playing with
lentils, and they threw them there, and a plant grew. So it cannot be contaminated"). And yet, despite the uncertainties, she knows, like the doctors at local
health center, that something is wrong in Flammable:

> On the weekends, when I go to my mom's in Wilde [a town about a half-
> hour away from Flammable], my kids sleep well, they sleep until 10 A.M., and
> they nap, and they sleep tight at night. Here they are always up early. They are
> always moving, nervous, as if they were tense. I sleep well there, too.

That "something" is making the children of Flammable sick, she believes. As
do many beneficiaries of the Plan Jefas y Jefes, she worked at the local health
center for a while. "All the kids there," she tells us, "have the same thing:
pimples, coughs, allergies.... I have these rashes in my back that I never had
before [the high-voltage wires were put up]. I'm taking antibiotics." Beliefs
about the effects of pollution come together with criticisms to the uses outsiders make of their suffering and with convictions regarding the actions of what
they see as the most powerful player in their lives, Shell.

**Verónica:** You know what happens? People are tired of all the deceiving talk [*de todo el chamuyo*]. They are tired of the photographer who shows up, takes a picture of your sick child, and then never comes back again....

**Javier:** Yes, and they are also tired of guys like me who come with a tape recorder....

**Verónica:** No. But they take the picture and...well, the company [*la empresa*, referring to Shell] buys them out. TV channels came here, and then the company bought them out so to prevent them from showing anything. What is more valuable? The money of Shell or the health of the children? There are a lot of sick children here.

Implicitly qualifying the dominant claims concerning poor "hygiene practices" as responsible for their poor health (while reproducing, in part, Shell's claim regarding the relationship between personal cleanliness and health), Verónica adds: "If you bathe your kid every day and you don't allow him to go to the dumping site, your child is not going to be infected. But there are kids who are sensitive to contamination, sensitive to all the garbage. They live with their legs all injured, with all those pimples and rashes. And their mothers don't have money to go to the hospital." Both Verónica and her brother Daniel are convinced that, when it comes to pollution, Shell silences even well-intended outsiders:

**Verónica:** Contamination was never an issue here before. [Reporters from] TV channels didn't come as they are coming now....

**Daniel:** No. Are you crazy? They, the guys from the Coast Guard [whom he sees as working for Shell] will not allow you to take pictures around here. If Sieppe finds out you are around, he will call you to his office and asks you how much you want to get out of here.

**Javier:** Sieppe? [Pretending not to know who this is.]

**Daniel:** Yes, the most powerful person at Shell....

**Verónica:** He is a mediator.

Verónica and Daniel think that the companies not only control whatever happens in the neighborhood but also are the ultimate arbiters of their lives: "They [the Brazilian oil company Petrobras] want us out of here by October. They bought this land because they want to have a parking lot here" (this conversation took place in July 2004; by September 2006, they were living in the same place and no relocation had occurred). And yet, despite all their suffering, their complaints, and their anxieties, Verónica and Daniel have hopes, all of them placed on their "wonderful lawyer. Thank God we have that lawyer, who came and saved us all." In a statement that summarizes her predicament, her thwarted waiting, her lack of trust in the state, and her expectations, Verónica tells us:

> Sometimes I don't want to wake up. And neither do they [referring to her three children]. But I understand them; it's all because of these wires. I didn't have them tested for contamination. I'm waiting for the lawyer to take us to a medical examination. If you do your examination in the local health center, the studies go to the municipality, and they get lost. I don't want my son to have a blood test every month, I don't want him to be hospitalized every three months and then to come back here. It's useless. So I am waiting for the lawyer to have us examined. Those exams are not going to get lost, and they are going to go straight to the judge. I have faith that we are going to leave this place. . . . I'm going to go to Tucumán, I'm going to go to the countryside. I'm leaving. I don't want to be here any more. When I'm somewhere else I'm okay, but every time I come back I get very annoyed because of all the dirt, the rats. I hate this neighborhood. I don't want to live here. I want something nice for my children.

Verónica's plight encapsulates many of the recurrent themes in Flammable toxic experience. We already examined some of them in the previous chapters: neighbors dislike their surroundings, they are uncertain about the concrete health effects of industrial pollution, they are frustrated with government inaction and suspicious of the compound's plants. Some other themes deserve closer scrutiny. In this chapter, we analyze the "case of the wires" as a failed collective attempt to address the issue of the environmental toxins. The case of the wires illustrates several other themes of Flammable toxic experience: the perceived overwhelming strength of the companies (who are seen as able to "purchase" everything) and the related weakness of residents (who believe that nothing can be done against rich companies that are in league with government authorities). The case of the wires will also serve us to introduce another crucial actor in the Flammable toxic experience: lawyers. Many residents have filed suit against Central Dock Sud for possible health harm created by the high-voltage line installed in 1999. Neighbors are not only waiting for social workers to send much needed aid, for doctors to resume the lead treatment, for hospitals to give them medicine, and for authorities to (possibly) relocate them. They are also waiting for lawyers to show up with news and judges to rule on their behalf.

## Seven Months in 1999: Exposure Protest

Mr. Nestor Ibarra
Programa Hoy por Hoy
Radio Mitre

Does anybody care if I survive?

My name is Débora Alejandra Swistun. I am twenty-one years old, and I am a student of anthropology at the National University of La Plata. I am also studying economics at the University of Buenos Aires. I took English and computing courses. I try to make ends meet with my family (two sisters, one brother, my mom, and my retired grandparents). . . . The reason I am writing is the following: this is a last attempt, a warning signal if you will, because I got tired of knocking on doors and of being underestimated by pseudo-politicians and bureaucrats.

I live in Flammable Shantytown. Does that name ring a bell? During the Alfonsín presidency, we survived the explosion of the *Perito Moreno*, an oil ship, which made us abandon our homes for fifteen days without anybody's help. A couple of years ago, a coke coal processing plant began to operate in the neighborhood. People all over the world have opposed it but our "generous" country agreed to it. Oil tanks, grease, gases, all sorts of fuels, and all kinds of pollutants, a hazardous waste incinerator, a landfill, and close to thirty plants. You might be asking whether this paradise where I eat, sleep, breathe, and try to make progress is located in some remote location, far away from civilization. My answer: I see it every day, I breathe it, I carry it inside of me. While I am sleeping, I am lulled by the explosions of the "monument to the match"—as we fondly call the chimney with that huge flame (since I was a kid, I was told that as long as the flame is on, we were safe) . . . .

As if all this were not enough, now they want to put a strawberry in the cake: a high voltage wire with 132,000 kw.

Are you interested in my humble future?

I want to finish my degree, I want a better life (and I am working to that end).... I know you are a sensible person, let me share my story and count on the support of your audience.

Débora A. Swistun
Gaona 2055 Dock Sud (1871)
Avellaneda
Buenos Aires

In July 1999, Débora wrote this letter to a prominent radio reporter (known for his "social sensibilities") in the hope of obtaining some public attention to what was then going on in Flammable: Since May, a group of neighbors, organized around SOFOMECO (the community improvement association) had put up a tent and were blocking the construction of the concrete pillars that would eventually end up supporting high-voltage wires (see Photos 5.2 and 5.3).

Residents were asking for the wires to have a different route (not on top of many homes) or to be put underground (a possibility that an engineer from Central Dock Sud, in a private conversation with Débora during a public meeting at SOFOMECO in 1999 defined as an "Oriental luxury"). Residents were afraid of accidents (because of the heavy traffic of flammable products in the area, they thought that the projected columns and wires might fall on their precarious houses) and of possible contamination (residents then and now believe that the electromagnetic field generated by the wires gives them headaches and skin rashes and might produce cancer and birth defects). In May 1999, the neighborhood witnessed the emergence of what we call, adapting from Adriana Petryna's notion of "biological citizenship" (2002) an exposure protest: a collective action in which people jointly made claims on the basis of a potential accident and/or disease.

A technical study conducted by a group of experts from the local university, the Ente Nacional Regulador de la Electricidad (ENRE), and the Central Dock Sud soon showed that the wires could not be placed underground given the network of pipelines lining the sandy soil of Flammable. Residents then began to demand a new route.

In the face of residents' collective determination (months went by, and participation in the "green tent" was still high), with dozens of people interrupting the attempts of workers to begin excavations, representatives from Central Dock Sud resorted to a divide-and-conquer strategy. The first offer came to the

**Photos 5.2 and 5.3** "Blockading 'the Wires.' Protest, 1999." (Photos taken by Débora Swistun)

neighborhood improvement association (which was organizing the block-ade) in the form of US $150,000 for public works. The neighborhood association rejected the offer. Sensing the growth of the community protest, the mayor, who was then running for reelection, offered to relocate the residents of Barrio Porst: the four blocks would be moved to one block somewhere in Wilde. The association rejected the proposal (the mayor "wanted these four blocks to be relocated in only one," neighbors remembered). One day, a few residents from Danubio and Porst were offered compensation for the nuisances that high-voltage towers would cause. Soon others began receiving similar offers. By November, eighty-three families had accepted between US $10,000 and US $20,000. All but seven families signed an agreement allowing the work to proceed. Those seven families were the object of immediate threats and harassments coming from some members of families who had signed the agreement. The reason was simple enough: no one would receive the money unless neighbors ceased their opposition, something that eventually happened when, seven months after the first protest, a group of residents in a public fight that some still shamefully remember took the green tent down against the will of the small group who had not signed the agreement. After months of (some public, some secret) negotiations, the ENRE and the municipality ended up approving the installation of the high voltage wires in Flammable.

Eighty-three families received the "compensation" from Central Dock Sud in three installments: 25 percent when the digging began (the day after the "green tent" was removed), 25 percent when the concrete columns were built, and the remaining 50 percent when the wires were put up. Some of the homes were moved to make room for the concrete towers but were later moved back to their former location (one result of which, as can be seen in Figure 5.1, are homes whose front yards face the concrete pillars). Many residents enjoyed the brief moment of conspicuous consumption that followed the installation of the wires. Many remember who bought a new car, a television, a computer, and/or a refrigerator.

The seven families that did not sign the agreement took the case to the courts. In the years that followed, other families contacted (or better, were contacted by) lawyers and are now suing Central Dock Sud for the alleged harm (present and future) caused by the wires. All of them are waiting; some, like Verónica and her brother Daniel, remain hopeful. They see the lawsuit as their ticket out of Flammable and their lawyers as their saviors.

### Fast Forward to 2005: Enter the Lawyers

Damián Fernandez is a young lawyer. He met Verónica and her brother Dani in the courts when they were acting as witnesses in a traffic accident case involving a friend. They got Damián and his partner interested in the case of the high-voltage wires when they mentioned that many families in the neighborhood had become sick because of the wires. Dani and Verónica remember that the two lawyers visited the neighborhood and were quite shocked when they saw the short distance separating the high-voltage pillars from the houses. "The people in the neighborhood," Damián says, "told us about the effects of the wires. . . . We didn't know anything . . . at the technical level, I mean, later we acquired that knowledge." Damián and his partner filed a lawsuit against Central Dock Sud; Edesur, the company that uses and distributes the electricity; and their insurance companies. They are asking for compensation for present and future (physical, psychological, and economic) harm caused by the high voltage wires.

When we ask him about the state of the lawsuit, he opens a filing cabinet and shows us the file that Central Dock Sud sent the judge: thousands of pages that will take weeks for him and his partner to review. "The defendants' lawyers belong to one of the two biggest firms in the country," Damián says. "We are fighting against a huge monster." This young lawyer says that he is not intimidated by his opponents' resources; that he wants—if not to win, something he suspects would be quite difficult—to reach an agreement that is "decent for neighbors and decent for us." In reference to the possibility of reaching an out-of-court agreement with the companies, Damián says, "We are not going to sell people out. We don't want to sell us out either. We want them to relocate the residents. But we want a good relocation. Not a relocation that moves them 40 kilometers away, or one in which neighbors lose all of their family networks. [If we are to achieve an agreement], it has to be a good and decent deal. We want residents to have a similar house in another place. And we want the companies to pay for all the damage they have caused."

Damián remembers that he and his partner began building their case "from scratch because, in terms of environmental rights, nobody knows anything. . . . First, we got a physician. We spent twelve hours a day in the neighborhood. The doctor checked everybody. The symptoms were very similar. They all have respiratory problems. He wrote up a brief clinical history of each resident. And we began to do research on the subject [on the health effects of electromagnetic fields]." He remembers that during six months, together with his partner and three assistants, they worked twelve hours a day, seven days a week and adds, not without some hope, "If all goes well, we'll get paid. If it doesn't, we'll get nothing." He mentions the titles of articles that they read (some published in the *American Journal of Epidemiology*), of the experts they consulted, and of one of court case in Spain that, he believes, is quite similar to the one they are trying to make.

His knowledge about the potential effects of electromagnetic fields (EMFs) on the health of the surrounding population is quite basic:

> We began to understand the effects of the electromagnetic fields on the body. On the basis of these scientific studies, we cannot assert that EMFs are harmful. But neither can we be certain that EMFs are harmless.... You end up knowing that, whether the EMFs cause harm or not, the possibility of harm is there. And this possibility increases because of the refineries and distilleries. A physician told us that the harmful effects of the EMFs grow with the lack of good nutrition.

Later he adds, without much empirical evidence as far as we can tell, that "the incidence of several types of cancer has increased among the people exposed to EMFs." Toward the end of our long conversation, he admits not knowing much in detail about the concrete health effects of electromagnetic fields but, in a statement that residents in Flammable would find plausible (and in a reasoning that resembles that of physicians at the local health center) he concludes: "I don't know what, but I am sure that they do something to people, something bad."

## Waiting

Flammable residents' long, impotent, and uncertain waiting is well illustrated in this dialogue with longtime residents García and Irma:

García: And now, we have to wait for Shell or someone else to push us out. Or maybe the municipality will expel us....

Débora: Who are they going to expel?

Irma: Us...

García: If they pay us, we leave....

Débora: And do you think they are going to pay us?

García: No, not really. Since 1982, there's a rumor that says that they are going to move us out.... But in this area everybody owns the property and it will cost them a lot of money...the people from

Danubio [where Verónica lives] will have to leave because the Bra-
zilians [referring to Petrobras] bought that piece of land, and they
are going to make a parking lot there.

Residents' experiences are very much permeated by this waiting—as we saw in
the previous chapter, since they live here they have been hearing rumors about
an imminent relocation. Lawyers and lawsuits now add another (more positive
but equally disempowering) layer to this "waiting time."

When it comes to the wires, residents hear something quite different from
what lawyers such as Damián say. The many times we talked with neighbors
about the wires they all said that "our lawyers told us that the wires are very
dangerous." When given the opportunity to portray what they dislike about
their neighborhood, school students point to the wires as the cause of their
own and their neighbors' illnesses: "Those wires produce cancer," they tell us.
The wires, Verónica and many others agree, are "making us sick." As Silvia,
another longtime resident says:

I had never had a headache, and I am forty-three years old. But everything
changes when they put up the wires. Since the wires went up, I have suffered from headaches; that thing totally changed me.

Ramiro, another old-timer, also has a bodily understanding of the effects of
the wires. As he puts it:

In the beginning [when the wires were put up], I felt a little bit...how do
I say this? The wires attack the brain, which is like a computer. I felt heavy, a
little bit dizzy. I studied myself. I was waking up as if I had a hangover. I then
realized that it was the wires. I never told my neighbors anything because
I don't want them to panic. But, you know, there are people here who get
sick, suddenly they get sick and they never suffered from anything.

As we saw in previous chapters, uncertainties, errors, and ignorance are widespread regarding the air, water, and soil contamination that originates in the
compound. When it comes to the wires, residents seem to approach a common viewpoint on their hazardous effects. The reason for that, we believe, is
twofold. First, unlike the long period of incubation of the pollution coming
from the compound, the wires were abruptly imposed on the population. Second, the wires triggered organized collective action and numerous lawsuits
that influenced the neighbors' collective representations. In residents' imagi-
nations, the high voltage wires embody both fear (of contamination and of an

accident) and hope (of winning a lawsuit). A successful lawsuit is seen as one of the few ways out of the neighborhood.

However, uncertainties die hard: they reappear when speaking about the lawyers and the lawsuits. Referring to the lawsuit against Central Dock Sud, Ramiro says, "We'll see what happens, to be honest, I don't know how far we are going to go with it. But we are going to get a solution.... The lawyer came this week [December 2005]. If she doesn't come again, I'll call her." The dialogue that ensued reflects Ramiro's waiting, which is filled with both hope and suspicion.

> **Débora:** Yes, you always have to be on top of the lawyers because if not...
>
> **Ramiro:** Yes, of course, you have to be on top of them...
>
> **Débora:** You have to call them, tell them how things are going. You should never stop calling them.
>
> **Ramiro:** Yes, but the lawyer has to push the paperwork because if not she will not get any money.
>
> **Débora:** Sure, but you also have to be calling her, showing your interest to her...
>
> **Ramiro:** Yes, but what if it's under the table? [referring to a possible deal that the lawyer might broker]
>
> **Débora:** But you trust her, don't you?
>
> **Ramiro:** Yes, but if she obtains a deal for herself she is never going to tell us...

## The Courts Rule

During the two and a half years of our fieldwork, Flammable neighbors have been awaiting news about the pending lawsuit and the always imminent relocation. They lived their lives, organized their daily routines, and established further roots in this poisoned place, all the while expecting something will soon change. News came, in the form of a court ruling, in late July 2006. What follows is an edited version of the fieldnotes we took during the last two weeks of that month. As the reader will see, the initial commotion created by the favorable court ruling was soon replaced by doubt and uncertainty. We decided to present the reader with our (slightly edited) fieldnotes to convey the process by which neighbors (and, to a certain extent, ourselves) are confused by a barrage of contradictory messages and interventions.

### Fieldnotes (Javier), July 12–July 26, 2006

As soon as I get to Débora's house today, she tells me that a lawyer came yesterday to meet Verónica and her neighbors. According to Verónica, the lawyer told the neighbors that in three or four months everybody is supposed to leave that area (which comprises twenty homes right beneath the high-voltage wire). The lawyer told the neighbors that a deal was made with the companies and that the latter will give money for residents to leave. Through Ramiro, who lives in this area, we find out that Damián Fernandez's partner, Dr. Zorilla, was the one who came yesterday to bring the news to all the families who are part of the lawsuit against Central Dock Sud. Verónica is not at home, but we find Karina Olmos (whose child Luisa is lead-poisoned [see chapter 3]) in her house. She had been at the meeting with the lawyer. She tells us that the lawyer showed them "a piece of paper signed by three judges.... The companies will pay us to leave. In three or four months we should go.... They will give us the money, and we'll leave." We ask her how much money she expects. She hesitates. "I hope they pay us ... so that we can leave," she says and adds: "Let's hope for the best.... The companies want this area to build a parking lot" (and it is pointless to tell her that right beside her property there's a huge piece of land that might serve that purpose and is currently deserted). When speaking about the lawsuit she oscillates back and forth between the damage caused by lead poisoning and the presumed effects of the electromagnetic field produced by the high-voltage wires. She doesn't actually know the specifics of the court ruling but believes it is all about the high-voltage wires—though she immediately adds "and the whole lead thing." ...

After several attempts I speak on the phone with Dr. Zorilla. She tells me that the courts have produced a preventive ruling (una medida cautelar) "to stop electropollution" in the neighborhood. I ask her about a timeline (the three or four months neighbors have in mind), and she tells me there's nothing decided yet. I ask her who is going to pay for the relocation. She doesn't know. In the lawsuit she "included everything in ... lead, the wires ... everything ... I put everything in" (yo metí todo junto). No wonder the neighbors are confused! "The lawsuit is about present and future damage, but it is almost impossible to get money from the insurance companies ..." Puzzled [because now I don't really understand what the neighbors are excited about], I ask her what will happen to residents: "When will they have to move out? What will happen to them?" Her answer illuminates the interplay of interests in which

Flammable residents' future is not the top priority: "Listen...I am neither Mother Theresa nor Chiche Duhalde [the wife of the former governor of Buenos Aires known for her charitable work for the poor]." What she, the lawyer, wants is a monetary compensation for the damage created by the contamination; if the residents get money (any money) she will receive a part of it, "and I make a living. Things worked out well for me so far..." She admits that to "prove" in court the damage created by the EMFs is a very difficult task. She hopes, as much as her partner did a year ago, to achieve some sort of settlement that will benefit both her and the neighbors in economic terms....

Débora gets a copy of the actual ruling from Eugenio, the former vice president of the improvement association. We read it hoping to find out whether or not the judges have ruled on behalf of the neighbors (and, also hoping to understand where the misinformation is coming from). It is an eleven-page document (expte n.7391/04, *Alarcón, Francisco y Otros c/Central Dock Sud S.A. y Otros s/Daños y Perjuicios. Cese de contaminación y perturbación ambiental*) filled with technical details and juridical jargon in which the preventive measure asked by the litigants—an immediate halt in the use of the high-voltage power lines—is, in fact, denied. The judges order the companies "within the next 120 days" to "take new steps" to "prevent the possible harm caused by electro-pollution." The judges ask the litigants to "reach an agreement" that might include relocation to places where the residents agree to move. The 120-day deadline is for the companies to present to the courts "a detailed report of the achieved outcomes."

What the courts actually rule differs quite remarkably from what the lawyers tell the neighbors and even more so from what the neighbors understand. I bet four months from now Verónica, Luisa, her lead-poisoned child, and the rest will still be living in the same place (maybe with some more money in their pockets, never enough to buy a place elsewhere). But I might be wrong. Maybe this time, residents will get enough money to purchase a home elsewhere.

Over lunch, Elsa (Débora's mother) asks me: "Do you think that this time something will happen? Or will it be as I said the other day, when I was talking like an old woman saying that they are about to relocate us? What do you think?" And I don't know what to tell her. Part of me knows that, without organized efforts on the part of the affected, not much will occur. But part of me hopes that this time something good might happen (compensation for damage, relocation, or both). I think I am beginning to share their (unfounded?) hopes. But, what if this time...?

## How Submission Works

If we decided to keep this long fieldnote in its raw form is not only because it describes action in real time and space (as many of those we interjected in the text so far do) but also because it gives a sense of how confusion and doubts (those of neighbors and, increasingly, our own) proceed. If the reader pays close attention, she might note that this fieldnote also reveals that, by the time we took it, we ourselves were trying to avoid Tiresias's fate of being "mere onlookers." On the contrary, we were quite explicitly, like the tuberculosis patients analyzed by Julius Roth (1963), demanding a timetable.

Initially residents' hopes are raised: Everybody we meet during those first two or three days after the lawyer came to the neighborhood is talking about relocation and also about possible sums of money ("Will it be 30,000 (US $10,000) or 50,000 pesos (US $16,600)?" "I will not move for 20,000 pesos (US $6,600)! No way!" "What if we ask 80,000 (US $26,600)?" we heard several times). As Maria tells us, "we will have to start looking for houses to buy." Two weeks later, doubts and confusion (as to what the judges actually said, and as to what is the lawyer is really trying to accomplish) settle. Although we began our fieldwork two and a half years ago when neighbors in this same area were saying that in the following three months everybody was supposed to leave, and we now know that "imminent removal" is part of what living in Flammable is all about, we somehow begin to share the hopes of residents. What if this time around this lawyer gets "it" (the "it" being an undefined mix of relocation and indemnification)? Shouldn't we wait to write our manuscript to report what really happens?

Regardless of what actually happens with the residents living under the high voltage wires, with those property owners living in the old part of Flammable (sarcastically called "*área premium*" by Shell), or with those in the new one (that, as municipal authorities inform us in August 2006, will be relocated within the next two years)—and as important as these developments are— we think that what is even more interesting, in socioanthropological terms, is what our tempography reveals about how submission works and how it is experienced. It works through yielding to the power of lawyers, judges, state officials. It is experienced as a waiting time: waiting (while becoming hopeful and then frustrated) for others to make decisions over their lives; surrendering themselves, in effect, to the authority of others. True, as poor, unemployed or underemployed people living in a highly contaminated no-go area, they are powerless to begin with. But in the past, during those months of the "exposure protest" described above, they did witness their own collective power. They also realized that "the monster" is quite powerful and that joint action has its implicit difficulties. As Débora (herself an activist back in 1999) asks in her fieldnotes reporting a meeting she had with the neighbors of Barrio Porst to discuss possible relocation alternatives: "What if we organize, we act collectively, and then people end up making their own private dealings as it happened when we fought against the power lines?"

Relocation and compensation for all the physical, psychological, and economic damage created by environmental contamination are indeed essential. If Luisa and the many other afflicted children are relocated to an area where they can play on clean ground, drink good water, and breathe fresh air, and if their families receive enough money to pay for lead treatments, their lives will dramatically improve. As concerned citizens (and, for Débora, as a neighbor), we both believe that relocation and compensation will make a crucial difference in their lives. And we hope that both will happen soon. But for us as analysts, what is at stake is different: we believe that whether or not they are relocated or compensated will have little effect on the dynamics of domination that shape their lives: residents in Flammable are condemned to live in a time oriented to and by others. In interesting and unexpected ways, then, the world of Tiresias finds parallels in the lives of contemporary shantytown dwellers who, like the Greek seer, are forced to become "mere onlookers." Destitute and poisoned Tiresias of the shanty world are living in a time dictated by others, an alienated time, obliged, as Pierre Bourdieu (2000:237) so eloquently puts it, "to wait for everything to come from others."

Even if the particular (and to a certain degree, extreme) relationship between time, behavior, and domination analyzed above is peculiar, to an extent, to Flammable, their intimate connection is a general phenomenon applicable, we believe, to all powerless groups living in territories of urban relegation. But in Flammable this dominated wait takes an exaggerated form and we have been noticing all the behaviors and opinions that manifest this exercise of power: neighbors' appointments with lawyers are constantly deferred, their lead screenings and other blood tests ("contamination exams" would be a better term) routinely delayed, their hopes falsely raised. Meanwhile, they wait. And, while they wait, the doubts about what others are presumably doing on their behalf grow. These doubts eventually become self-doubts about their own (individual and collective) power. As we repeatedly heard over two and a half years: "You can't fight against that monster..." "What if we organize and then they all sell out?" Their beliefs about their own collective capacities constitute the subject of the next chapter.

# 6

## Collective Disbelief in Joint Action

Flammable contains many of the elements—contamination of air, water, and soil; deterioration of public hygiene; a housing crisis—of what Manuel Castells (2002:ix) calls "the dark side of the urbanization process." In this urban dystopic world, is it possible to find a trajectory that counteracts the many misinterventions and that clarifies rather than obscures the sources and effects of poisoning? As we will describe below, we began this project with the theoretical possibility of alternative collective agency in mind. Imagining the possibility of joint action is simple but, as Peter Evans states (2002:13), "constructing a clear picture of who might exercise such agency and how is more complicated. Who are the potential agents of livability?" In this chapter we examine the neighborhood as a potential site of collective mobilization against environmental suffering.

Typically, risk frames of the kind we analyzed in previous chapters are used as an independent variable to explain the collective actions people take to protest, and protect themselves, against toxic hazards (see Tierney 1999; Brown and Mikkelsen 1990; Beamish 2001; Lerner 2005). Although the general uncertainty that we examined might be related to the collective quiescence that, as we will see, is quite apparent in the neighborhood, we have thus far not focused attention on this latter, and analytically different, phenomenon.[1] We have focused instead on the confused and mistaken beliefs people hold about danger as dependent variables inspecting the social origins of these perceptions.

In the scholarship on social movements and contentious politics, there is no generalizable connection between participation and consciousness or, more specifically, collective action and certainty. Protest might be the consequence (but also the cause) of increasing critical awareness or knowledge (for different arguments, see Tilly 1978; McAdam 1982; Snow and Benford 1988; Tarrow 1998; Mansbridge and Morris 2001; Polletta 2006). This chapter will ethnographically explore the links between the socially produced toxic uncertainty and collective action in the hope that such analysis will further our comprehension of the connections between perceptions of danger and mobilization. We will see that collective understandings and joint action establish a recursive relationship. We also hope that by the end of this chapter the reader will have a better grasp on the reasons why Flammable residents are not acting collectively on their shared grievances.

## To Leave or Not to Leave

As we began our fieldwork in May 2004, we read in the newspapers that some 150 families from Villa Inflamable were squatting on public land to force the local government to "give us land so that we can move out of Flammable" (*Pagina12*, May 27, 2004). "We are surrounded by pollution," neighbors told reporters, "we have the Riachuelo on one side, a canal that brings industrial waste from the petrochemical compound on the other, and a web of pipes carrying chemicals beneath us. We are standing on top of a bomb." We thought we had what sociologists call a "paired comparison" in progress: On equally contaminated grounds, some families were leaving the neighborhood in an organized way, whereas other families were staying. Intrigued as we were about the meanings of pollution, we thought the natural experiment would allow us to add a "collective action" focus to our research: How and why were some neighbors organizing against toxic assault and demanding new land while the majority was staying behind seemingly without complaint?

News reports were quite misleading. Not only did they misrepresent the numbers of Flammable families living in the neighborhood (and mobilized during the squatting) and the name of the neighborhood (*Crónica*, for example, called it Villa Emplomada—"Leaded Shantytown" [May 27, 2004]) but, most important, they wrongly portrayed the land invasion as an outcome of the joint action of Flammable neighbors. It was, we learned a few weeks later, a squatting action jointly organized by some radical activist groups to obtain concessions (land, among them) from the local government. Among participants were only a few Flammable residents. Despite the failed comparison, the general concern with the likelihood of protest or other type of collective action (squatting, for example) stayed with us. Why, we frequently asked ourselves, do not neighbors complain publicly *and collectively* about their situation? With the exception of the "case of the wires" in 1999 and some brief community opposition to the opening of the coke processing plant in 1995, there was not much locally generated protest against contamination. Why?

This general concern permeated much of our inquiry into the social production of the experience of contamination. It reemerged as a focus of specific attention toward the end of our fieldwork, when official talks of relocation and lawyers' presence (and court rulings) became part of daily conversations. What would neighbors do if the local state carried out its promised relocation plans?

On June 2006, the Supreme Court of Argentina ordered the national government, and the governments of the state of Buenos Aires and of the City of Buenos Aires, to present a plan for the cleanup of the Riachuelo. As we said in chapter 1, Villa Inflamable sits right on the banks of the mouth of this highly polluted river. The Supreme Court, furthermore, ordered forty-four companies (among them Shell, Petrobras, and Central Dock Sud) to report on their waste-processing programs. The Supreme Court responded in this way to a demand presented by several lawyers on behalf of 140 neighbors of Dock Sud. The lawyers also asked for the creation of a compensation fund for the "victims of contamination" who, according to the text of the lawsuit, suffer lead poisoning, congenital malformations, and spontaneous abortions.[2] Although the Supreme Court ordered the companies and the different governments to provide reports and plans, it did not produce a ruling with respect to the compensation fund. The creation of the fund, the justices argued, was defined as a matter for district judges.

María del Carmen is one of the residents of Flammable who is a litigant in this lawsuit. Since the first time pollution was raised as an issue to be reckoned with in Flammable, she has been outspoken about its pernicious health effects, mainly, but not exclusively, on two of her children. On January 1, 2002, a report in *Clarín* titled "Thirty Blocks from the Obelisc [monument at the center of downtown Buenos Aires], an Area with Rare Chemical Odors," was the first to portray María del Carmen's plight:

> María del Carmen Brite's house stands in the middle of the Petrochemical Compound. She shows us the x-rays of the damaged lungs of her daughter, Camila, who is four years old. Camila has serious respiratory problems. Her clinical story indicates fetal suffering due to the inhalation of acid. And her brother, Emir, has his legs marked by huge, dark rashes.

Four and a half years later, the same newspaper, in a report titled "Life in the Riachuelo: 'We Are Slowly Dying,' " portrays the Brite family still living in Flammable. "This is only an allergy," she says, referring to the rashes that still plagued Emir (who by then was ten). "We don't know what's going on inside him." In an earlier conversation, she told us that "Emir is full of pimples, he can't wear shorts. He looks like a *sarnoso* [someone with scabies]. I can't take him to a swimming pool because they won't allow him there." Referring to the recent Supreme Court ruling, María del Carmen tells *Clarín* reporters: "We do not want money. We only want them to pay for the treatments. We are slowly dying here."Although most neighbors recognize María del Carmen as a blunt, defiant, and always active person in matters of Flammable's pollution, not everybody would agree with her statements regarding possible solutions to the problem. As lawyers' presence and talks of relocation increase, so do neighbors' disagreements regarding what to demand and from whom. In a meeting at the local improvement association in October 2006, neighbors from Barrio Porst agree that they do not want to be part of the state "housing program" that seems to be about to begin—the municipal government had recently announced a plan to relocate three hundred families to a new housing complex. They disagree, however, in exactly what they want and where they should lodge their claims. During the last few months of our fieldwork, we heard people say, "The municipality should give us US $80,000 to buy a new house," "Shell should buy us out...they have the money," "We should ask money from Shell so that we can buy a house elsewhere," "The lawsuit will bring us enough money to allow us to buy us something." We also heard some people repeatedly state that they, unlike the shantytown dwellers, owned their land and homes and that these are worth an important amount of money. Paraphrasing the *Communist Manifesto*, we could say that many old-time residents, far from perceiving they have nothing to lose but their (poisoned) chains, think that demanding relocation might end up destroying the most valuable possession they have: their homes. In the many conversations we had with them—and in their statements at meetings in the local improvement association—they seemed unsure whether they want to leave. It is, true, our interpretation. They do not say it quite so. The many "buts" they raise every time relocation is discussed—the many conditions they would like to see met before even thinking about moving out—make us think that old-timers want to remain in Flammable. As Débora wrote in one of her fieldnote entries after one such meeting at the local improvement association: "This meeting was very frustrating. Sometimes I am not sure if they want to leave or not."

Be that as it may, one thing is clear: residents place all their hopes in what the government, the companies, or lawyers and judges will do *on their behalf*, not on what they can jointly achieve (significantly, many of the meetings we attended ended with neighbors agreeing to request a meeting with the mayor, Shell personnel, or the secretary of public works). Collective action of the contentious kind was never raised as possibility when news concerning court rulings and rumors about impending relocation plans were running rampant. As defiant as María del Carmen and many others at the local improvement association seem to be, they see others, not themselves, as the engines of change. Theirs is a hopeful submission to both degraded living conditions and to the actions of others.

At the same time, residents of Flammable are hardly passive. When, during the course of our fieldwork, rumors about relocation triggered meetings at the local improvement association, the participants' behavior belied any simplistic assertion about collective inaction. In what follows we present a brief description of one such meeting. The course of the meeting, what was said and left unsaid, condense what we believe is a general problem in the association's recurrent attempts to organize and mobilize residents: namely, it is quite difficult for them to agree on what they want to achieve—a common "frame" in the language of social movement scholarship. And, furthermore, they lack confidence in their own collective energy. Disagreement and distrust in shared efficacy feed and reinforce each other.

Eugenio, vice president of the local improvement association, is a member of the small but active Socialist Party. In April 2006, he told six residents who had gathered at his house for a meeting that he had informed party representatives to the National Congress (a senator and a deputy) of the situation in Flammable. Eugenio says that legislators told him "we should present a proposal, and they will fight for it. Because there are funds, there's money.... They told me that we should get together, and learn how to struggle together." Eugenio told the neighbors present at the meeting that he is convinced that if the legislators of the Socialist Party had a proposal signed by the neighbors, "something will happen ... there are funds available." "We need to ask for relocation in a place that is habitable," he said. "But not everything is the same.... There are people who own their homes, there are other who have only been here for a couple of years." Some of those attending wanted to know exactly where they would be moved to. Eugenio told them that they would need to insist on the same "amenities" they have in Flammable. They could demand a lump sum, he said, but that's "up to the lawyers." Even when he himself is unclear as to what the petition should demand (relocation to a new housing project or relocation to houses selected by neighbors or a lump sum of money so that residents can themselves buy a place), he insists that they should "come to an agreement ... because this is a great opportunity—we have someone who supports us." Eugenio does not mention the obvious fact that this support is marginal—the Socialist Party has only a handful of representatives in both congressional chambers—and seems enthusiastic at the prospect of circulating a petition and getting the political process going.

Walter, who lives in a house across the entrance of Shell refinery, was one of the six people at the meeting. He had recently learned that Shell is buying land in the neighborhood. "Shell is slowly buying some plots of land," he told the group. "Shell is invading the neighborhood," he said. The meeting then takes a sudden turn and residents begin to talk about what they think the company is planning to do in Flammable. "They are going to build another plant to make gasoil," Walter states. "They want to build a parking lot, for two thousand trucks..." Susana asserts. "They want to build another dock, for big ships," Eugenio says he has heard from other neighbors. Walter then matter-of-factly states: "They want us to move out...but they don't want to put out any money. Something is brewing...I am not leaving. I'd like to leave with my family, because the kids are the ones who are absorbing all this [contamination]. But we have to stay put." Eugenio replies, "If there's money, I'll do business." Susana says, "If there's money, we'll all leave." The conversation then moves to the amount of money they would accept for moving out: sums oscillate between 25,000 and 80,000 thousand dollars. Eugenio adds: "We need to do something. We are dying because of contamination. They have to do something about it. We need to make a proposal." Neighbors then talk about where they would go "with the money we get." Some say they will go back to the province that they came from, others that they will move close by because "there's work here." The meeting ends with Eugenio asking them to tell other neighbors to come to the next meeting, so that "we can see what they want and write a petition."

This two-hour-long meeting is then followed by other meetings (quite similar in content and sequence). Those attending agree that contamination is a problem, but disagree on what they should do about it. The main disagreement could be stated as follows: Should they demand relocation or money to buy their homes elsewhere? If they demand relocation, will property owners be relocated together with shanty dwellers? If they ask for money, how much will they accept to leave? These meetings are also characterized by two other main elements: (1) Participants typically move from what they would like to what they think the compound companies are (secretly) planning to do with them; and (2) they don't touch the issue of compensation for past and present harm caused by contamination. This is never raised as an issue that demands their collective action. In our own experience, the second point admits a single exception: we once heard Juan Carlos say, "It's not a matter of packing and leaving. We first need to find out what we have in our bodies."

The misgivings neighbors who partake in these meetings have about their own collective capacity and efficacy are manifested in both the amount of time they devote to chatting about what they think companies such as Shell and Petrobras are plotting (talking endlessly about the powerful seems to be a way of conveying their own powerlessness) and in the usual agreements that neighbors reach at the end of these meetings: requesting a meeting with this or that official or with Shell's neighborhood representative to obtain further information about what is being done to address the neighborhood's present and future condition. During these two years, neighbors did not plan a demonstration, a street blockade,[3] or any other transgressive form of contention. Demanding meetings with officials or with company personnel is the only performance available in their collective action repertoire; jointly claiming compensation for environmentally related health problems is not part of their collective discursive repertoire.[4] Neighbors end up relying for solutions on the same agents who are responsible for their suffering.

> I have lived here since 1955. I grew up here. I got my education here, got married here, had my children here. The people who live in these four blocks [the Barrio Porst] . . . we were born here, our folks died here and they left us here . . . It is not easy for me to leave. They have been talking about relocation for a long time. It never happened. Once I spoke with someone at Shell because there was a rumor going around saying that relocation was about to happen. He told me, "No, don't worry, you can stay there, nobody will move you out of there. We need land, but we need a lot of land, not those four blocks. We are expanding into the river." (Marga, president of the Local Improvement Association)

"Maybe, what has not happened in a hundred years, happens in one second," says Elsa, Débora's mother. She is referring to the possibility of the relocation recently raised by a municipal official (about which we read in the newspaper). That "maybe" conveys some hope. It also encapsulates one defining feature of residents' lack of belief in collective agency. If something occurs, it will be because of someone else's decision, not residents' own volition and action.

We began our fieldwork with the specter of collective action in mind, and we ended up with extensive notes that register its absence. We thus share Peter Evans cautious skepticism when he writes:

Despite the attractiveness of communities as alternative agents, the idea that neighborhoods of dis-privileged urban households might become agents of livability is audacious. The romantic vision that "community" automatically entails homogeneity and unity of purpose is misleading even in traditional rural settings; urban communities contain an even more daunting spectrum of interests, identities, and political positions. Communities also lack power. As long as they act by themselves, the capacity to reshape the larger urban environment is beyond them. (2002:15)

Flammable's lack of collective action may be explained by a number of factors that converge and reinforce one another: a lack of networks linking neighbors with outside influential actors, the (up until recently) absence of opportunities for environmental claim making, the scarce resources for mobilization at neighbors' disposal, and disbelief in their own joint capacities. The nature of their grievances (neither suddenly imposed nor abruptly realized but gestated in a slow and dispersed form) and the way they interact with networks, opportunities, resources, and frames (and we should here include the discursive interventions of other actors which act as counter-frames) might also help to comprehend acquiescence and the way it ends up reinforcing generalized uncertainty and confusion.[5]

Although it is difficult for us to fully understand and explain collective inaction, we should note that this is not, we believe, related to the structural situation of Flammable residents—which leads us to qualify Evans's generalizing assertion quoted above. Two elements show that there is nothing inherent in the powerlessness of poor communities that in and of itself can explain the recursive relationship between widespread toxic uncertainty and lack of mobilization. First, some of the most confused and/or mistaken residents are found among residents of Flammable who are least poor: those living in the oldest part of the neighborhood. Second, nearby contaminated communities, which are as powerless and as poverty-stricken as Flammable, have gone through the process of increasing critical awareness (through a version of popular epidemiology) that evolved into massive protests against toxic assaults (for a recent example of collective action in response to the discovery of a leukemia cluster in a close by poor neighborhood, see Merlinsky 2007b; for another example of dispossessed neighbors acting collectively against toxic assault in the United States, see Lerner 2005).

Before we conclude this chapter, a final nuance is in order. As we wrapped up the fieldwork component of this book, Javier was interviewed by the newspaper

*Página/12.*[6] With the title "En los estudios de pobreza el medio ambiente ha sido rezagado" [In the studies of poverty, the environment is relegated], the interview caught the attention of the about to be sworn-in federal undersecretary of sustainable development (who was to become an official at the federal Department of Environment) who contacted Javier the same day the interview was published. She asked Javier if he or someone he might recommend would be willing to join the state agency under her command. Javier declined (he has not resided in Argentina since 1992 and was scheduled to leave the country in less than a month) but put this official in touch with Débora as someone with firsthand experience on environmental issues. Since then, Débora has worked as an advisor at the revamped federal Department of Environment (Secretaría de Medio Ambiente y Desarrollo Sustentable). Her main task has been to push for a massive relocation of Flammable (a plan that includes, among other things, the creation of a fund with money from the federal government and the petrochemical companies to subsidize new homes and health care for the entire population) and a cleanup program for the area around the petrochemical compound. Débora's are not solo efforts. For the past year, the agency has received massive funding from the federal government and has been pursuing new environmental initiatives (the clean-up of the Riachuelo, the monitoring and sanctioning of contaminating industries, etc.). It is still too early to assert whether or not these plans will be successful, and a full chronicle of Débora's actions and the resistance they encountered (a veritable ethnography of state policy-making) is beyond the scope of this book. All we can do is highlight the fact, well-known to urban theorists (Evans 2002), that the problems of environmental (un)livability will not be solved by maverick individual actions: They are collective problems and must be resolved collectively.

The work of Peter Evans and his collaborators (2002) is again of analytical help: they counterpoise the grim diagnoses of communities' difficulties in challenging environmental degradation with instances of "state-society synergy"—occasions in which "engaged public agencies and mobilized communities enhance one another's capacity to deliver collective goods" (21) and with "jujitsu tactics"—"efforts to leverage the conflicts and contradictions that already exist within state apparatuses to shift the balance of state action toward livability" (236). The more recent work by Hochstetler and Keck (2007), in turn, describes many instances of cooperation ("enabling networks") between state actors and environmental activists in Brazil. Although the Argentine state is not usually reliable (and we have documented to the extent to which it has been in part responsible for Flammable's dramatic condition), agencies within it might work as potential allies. It is again too early to say whether some actions of the environmental agency (part of what Bourdieu would call, the "left hand of the state" [Bourdieu et. al 1999]) might break with local acquiescence and foster a surge of mobilization in Flammable. It is also premature to even speculate about what jujitsu tactics will have to be enacted to initiate positive change in the neighborhood. As difficult as it is, the case of Cubatao documented in Lemos (1998; see also Hochstetler and Keck 2007) and the many cases examined in Evans (2002) attest to the fact that the theoretical and empirical possibility does indeed exist.

# 7

## The Social Production
## of Toxic Uncertainty

Our long-term ethnography captures the collective construction of meanings and the making of (in)decisions, the waiting, in situ, as they unfold.[1] We were there when neighbors were wondering out loud about the possible short- and long-term effects of air, water, and soil pollution; when far-fetched rumors were running rampant and neighbors were evaluating the likelihood of this or that "imminent" relocation plan; and at the time when they were fantasizing about what they would do with the montón de plata (mountain of money) they would surely receive from the courts. We were also there at the time when all sorts of often contradictory material and symbolic interventions were molding people's perceptions of their surroundings: from the seemingly minor and inconsequential T-shirt with a corporate logo or a small fellowship to take a computer class inside the compound or a food program designed to teach neighbors to "eat well," to the disruptive appearances of star journalists and the broadcast of Flammable's plight on national TV, or the random visits of lawyers or officials and the ensuing high hopes continually raised among residents. We were there reading the newspaper and watching TV with residents when news about the relocation of some compound plants were announced and when municipal officials informed the public that "soon" hundreds of families were going to be moved out of the neighborhood. We were there when children's lead screenings were suspended and when they would soon (always soon) be restarted. Ours was not a retrospective reconstruction but an embedded form of inquiry in real time and space.

Once we ethnographically tilled the soil of existing meanings and behaviors related to surrounding contamination, we realized that pollution facts were sometimes overlooked (as is YPF's documented and sanctioned contribution to soil contamination) and other times misinterpreted (as with ideas about the spatial distribution of lead). When we investigated the reasons for this uncertainty and confusion, we ourselves stumbled and became less and less certain about what was going on, what had happened in the past, and what was about to happen. We were always interested in analyzing the meanings of contamination, but we became increasingly interested in establishing the basic facts about life in the shantytown. Did this official say that? Is the census that is being conducted related to a future eradication? Did the doctor actually tell you that you need to move out? Is your daughter showing signs of poisoning?

The aspects of the Flammable toxic experience that made us hesitate during the course of our fieldwork—What if this time this lawyer gets a favorable court ruling? What if this official is able to carry out this relocation plan? Are the lead-poisoned kids living in the lowlands? Is it possible that the same big companies that organize the distribution of aid in the neighborhood are responsible for its widespread poisoning?—are the same factors that explain how residents think and feel about pollution. We doubted not only because the links among location, contamination, and health are intrinsically ambiguous and/or contentious, even more so when the activities of big companies are involved (Phillimore et al. 2000), but also because *doubt was crafted* by many of the actors we interviewed for this project. Many times, these people exhibited certainty about things that admit scarce assurance and contradicted one another even on basic facts, such as the number of companies inside the compound, the type of emissions they produce, and the findings of the epidemiological studies recently conducted.

Flammable residents are exposed to a poisoned habitat; their understanding of that habitat is a confused and uncertain one. Confusion and uncertainty feed—and are fed by—their waiting and their submission. Why?

If we read the testimonies carefully and take a close look at residents' actions and inactions, we detect more or less accurate assumptions or tacit understandings about how companies behave; how politics works; what the medical profession is doing or not doing; how residents relate to company personnel, government officials, and other actors; and how they detect contamination in their own bodies. Together, these unspoken assumptions constitute "a repository of unarticulated source material from which self-conscious thought and action emerge" (Vaughan 1998:31); or, following Bourdieu, a repertoire of subjective, but not individual, schemes of perception, appreciation, and action. If we want to understand and explain why Flammable residents experience toxicity the way they do, we need to dissect the genesis of these collective schemes or frames that they use to understand and misunderstand what is going on.

Our analysis highlighted several factors that jointly shape these collective frames, and thus residents' dispositions toward the contaminated habitat. The uncertain material grounds—the constant threats of relocation, the disputes over who has administrative power over the territory of Flammable—have

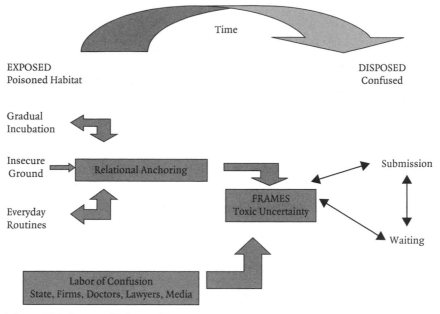

**Figure 7.1** "Exposed/Disposed"

undoubtedly shaped the frames through which people live and perceive themselves and their place. Uncertainty is a built-in element in the cultural repertoire of Flammable residents. Despite the shaky grounds, daily routines were never drastically disrupted. This lack of major disturbances contributed to the smooth operation of routines in what they do best: work as horses' blinders, enhancing focus on whatever the task at hand was and restricting their vision to (or camouflaging) the dangers that were increasingly being shaped outside of the immediate environment of their homes.[2] Routines as blinders are thus another shaper of the cognitive and evaluative structures through which people experience their environment. The many conversations and interviews we had with old-timers led us to think that routines were quite helpful in overcoming the uncertainty inherent in living in a place that has always been about to be vacated but that nobody has claimed jurisdiction over.

The familiar routines of going to work, sending kids to school, preparing meals, and putting babies to sleep have an ordering effect. They orient and stimulate action. They also have a comforting, almost soothing effect. We can count on routines and the interactions they involve to help us navigate difficult, uncertain moments: we find security in what is familiar to us, in what we can get a hold on; routines, furthermore, help us screen out or, at least, suspend the thought of the unpleasant. As routines provide us with a known route, with an "objective universe of incitements and indications" (Bourdieu 2000:222), they ground our existence. This latter aspect of routines' cultural work is quite relevant to understand older residents' experiences of contamination. In many of the life stories, in-depth interviews, and informal conversations we had with them, it became quite clear that they had been occupied with the same tasks that other recent migrants faced when first coming to Buenos Aires (finding work, building a home, forming a family, etc.). As their lives were filled up with these activities, their land, water, and soil were slowly being filled with pollutants. With the exception of the havoc created by the explosion of the *Perito Moreno* oil ship and with the trouble created by the installation of the high-voltage wires, daily routines were never interrupted: no major accidents occurred, and no generalized diseases that could be traced to activities in the compound were discovered, such as leukemia or other types of cancers that have incited people to act in other parts of the world. And since continuity was never dissolved—if anything, residents were, as many noted, "making progress" or as others put it "living our lives"—the routines ("working, always working") and relations ("we were all friends") *rooted* residents in Flammable.[3]

As threats of relocation waxed and waned and neighbors were busy building their homes and living their lives, contamination was slowly incubating in Flammable's water streams, soil, air, and in the bodies of its inhabitants. This temporal dispersion is a key factor in the molding of collective schemes. Here Diane Vaughan's detailed examination of the production and normalization of a cultural belief in risk acceptability within NASA finds interesting parallels in Flammable shantytown. Noting the absence of major disruptions and the gradual increment of seemingly minor problems in the space shuttle program, she writes:

> Had all the changes occurred at once, had damage been occurring on every flight due to a common cause, or had there been a discernable pattern of damage, the work group would have had some strong, clear signals with the potential to challenge the cultural belief in risk acceptability. Instead, the damage occurred incrementally, each incident's significance muted by social context and a learning-by-doing approach that had engineers interpreting each episode as separate and local. (1998:38)

It was, to quote an informant in Lynn Eden's penetrating analysis of thinking about fire damage in American nuclear planning since World War II, a "continuing pileup of things" (2004:271). That "continuing pileup of things" shapes the way planners incorporate (or fail to incorporate) fire effects into standard models of nuclear damage, gives form to the ways in which NASA personnel think about risk, and molds the confused ways in which Flammable residents think and feel about their environment: not in the ways an outsider would, but in the *situated* form that emerges from a long incubation period.

Residents did not abruptly "discover" that their neighborhood was polluted; no alarm suddenly went off, no warning was signaled, no "tipping point" was reached "when impressions of what was normal quickly changed" (Beamish 2000:481). Lead, benzene, toluene, and all sorts of chemicals gradually accumulated in the ground, streams, and bodies. In other words, Flammable residents' schemes of perception are, much like those of scientists and other professionals within highly specialized organizations, embodied history; their collective frames are "the active presence of the whole past of which [they are] the product" (Bourdieu 1977:56).

Perceptions about the toxic environment should thus be analyzed as products of individual and collective biographies, as sedimentations of actors' previous place-based experiences (Schutz 1962; Bourdieu 2000). Toxic beliefs or, to put it in phenomenological terms, toxic experiences, are *anchored* in the interactions and routines that characterize a particular place. But perceptions of hazards are also manipulable, susceptible of being molded by the practical and discursive interventions of powerful actors (Williams 1977; Thompson 1984; Heimer 1988; Bourdieu 1991; Perrow 1999). The stock of knowledge that people have about their surroundings at a particular time and place is therefore a joint product of the history of that place, the routines and interactions of its residents, and the power relations in which they are enmeshed. In the production of toxic uncertainty, the relational anchoring of risk perceptions meets the labor of confusion performed by influential actors.

The past then weighs in the development of the classificatory schemes of Flammable residents. And so do present material and symbolic interventions—the final main factor molding Flammable collective frames. Some of these interventions, such as Shell's charity, physicians' approach to contamination-related illnesses as unrelated to the environment, and the state's "averted gaze" are reproductive: they reinforce the dominant confusion. Others are Janus-faced: the deeds and words of lawyers, media, and some state officials perpetuate confusion but also have the potential to introduce other symbolic forms that might counteract the insufficient and inaccurate information broadcasted by powerful institutional forces. In both cases, however,

Flammable residents exercise scarce, if any, control on which information, which reasons, which stories reach them.

Although our analytic focus is on the production of uncertainty and not on the inability to anticipate and identify worst-case scenarios, some of the "interventions" we described are akin to the practices that initiate and sustain what Karen Cerulo calls positive asymmetry: "a way of seeing that foregrounds or underscores only the best characteristics and potentials of people, places, objects, and events" (2006:6). In collectively performing the labor of confusion, government officials, doctors, corporate personnel, and lawyers engage in what Cerulo labels "eclipsing" (rendering the most damaging aspects of life in Flammable invisible, as when Shell agents and doctors deny the existence of contamination-related illnesses), "clouding" (as when state actors keep the diagnosis of pollution and its attendant solution vaguely defined), and "prescriptive recasting" (as when lawyers redefine the worst—e.g., "having shit in your drinking water"—as a good "because you can get a lot of money out of it").[4]

In a nutshell, Flammable residents' experiences of their polluted surroundings are socially and politically determined. They do not follow straightforwardly from the toxic environment but from schemes of perception, appreciation, and action that have been shaped by history and by the present discursive and material interventions. These frames are, in other words, structured and structuring: they shape what people see, what they don't see, what they know, what they don't know, and what they would like to know, what they do and what they don't do.

Before concluding, let us make a brief reflexive turn, a sort of self-analysis, to inspect the ways in which the relationship between being exposed and being disposed that we have thus far dissected operates in the life of Débora—the resident researcher or native anthropologist.

## The Sad Truth

When Débora's grandfather, Antonio, got seriously ill, many old-time friends came to visit him. Damián Siri was among them. Débora spent hours drinking *mate* and talking with him about the history and the present of Flammable. He lived here from 1950 until two years ago, when he moved a fifteen-minute drive away. He knows Flammable's history in detail. We decided to present this edited version of her five-hour-long conversation because, on the one hand, Siri clearly articulates some of the views and evaluations of many old-timers.

Siri, for example, links contamination to government corruption, sees the changes in the neighborhood as a combination of increasing environmental degradation and everyday violence whose source is the nearby shantytown, and conflates (much as lawyers do) the toxicity of lead with that of the high-voltage wires. At the same time, he ascribes to some of the folk theories about pollution that residents hold and reproduce. He disagrees, however, with some of the views held by his former neighbors. Oil is here seen as a benign thing and YPF, which in the recent past was forced to clean the toxic sludge it had dumped in Flammable, is perceived as a "good mother" and, like some residents' views of Shell, as "the best company in the world." As we said at the beginning of chapter 3, we choose to display Siri's point of view in full not to throw doubt on the points of views of others but because it plainly shows the existing disagreements. This long interview, furthermore, ended with a warning to Débora, a warning that would soon become a dire premonition. To guide the reader toward the several relevant features present in Siri's story, we added headings taken from phrases in the interview.

### "It Was Very Peaceful Here"

"This was full of small farms...all small farms up to the shore. It was very peaceful. You could sleep with your door open. You could leave your bicycle outside, you could even forget about it and nobody would touch it. During summertime, people use to walk to the coast. The buses were full. There was a park, full of trees, and you could stay all day long, have a barbecue, eat there. The shore is now all polluted....I remember that there were crabs on the beach, the water was crystal-clear. I used to go to drink my *mates* there....When I was a kid, you could drink the water in the farms, you could swim in the beach. The fish was so tasty, it was much better than the one you would by in the super-market. The fauna was extraordinary...frogs, oysters, otters. People from all over Buenos Aires used to come here to spend the day. It was beautiful. Nobody would steal anything; as I said, you could sleep with your door open."

### "It's Not the Oil"

"Oil is not the problem. It doesn't harm anybody because it stays on the sur-face of the river, and it doesn't mix with the water. What companies throw to the river is much worse than that. It's sulfuric acid, lead. It all comes together in the bottom of the river and it poisons the fish. For the past hundred years there've been oil companies here and this was a garden, a beautiful garden with no contamination. You could drink water from the open ditches and it was OK.

The oil companies never contaminated here. Oil is not dangerous, because it stays on the surface. [Pollution comes from] the Compañía Química. It dumps something like 80 tons of sulfuric acid into the Río de la Plata. That's the water that people drink. The waste that the Compañía Química throws to the river mixes with the water."

### "The Companies Spend Money Bribing Politicians and Keep Poisoning the People"

"I am not afraid of saying this. Politicians give permission to the Compañía Química to stay here because of the huge bribes.... Now the neighborhood is all polluted because there are interests at stake. If the government really wanted to, they could order the companies to stop dumping all the waste in the river.... The companies spend money bribing politicians and keep poisoning the people.... We are all drinking the water from the Río de la Plata. That water is so polluted it cannot be purified. In the long run, you get sick. The rich people drink mineral, bottled water. They are not interested in the poor. The poor are those who always put in the effort to build up this country. Politicians should do something about all this. They should stop receiving bribes. If they want money, they should go to work."

### "YPF Was My Second Mother"

"I don't think there's another company in the world like YPF. She [referring to YPF] was like my second mother. I've never seen a better company. I got paid every 24th of the month. They would never fire you, unless you do something terrible like getting drunk or get into a fight. They gave you clothes, shoes.... If you worked extra hours, they would pay you very, very well, and always on time.... If I were healthier and younger, I would go back to YPF. I would work for YPF only for the food, because that company has been very good to me. I bought my house with the money I made there, I bought two new cars.... A lot of people live quite well because of YPF."

### "There Are a Lot of Bad People in the Shantytown"

"The neighborhood is in very bad shape now. I have nothing against the poor but...I see that the shantytown has grown. And there are good people in the shantytown, but there's a high percentage of bad people there. They come from other places, they steal, and they take refuge there.... The neighborhood is ugly now...besides all the contamination.... Very bad people hide in the shantytown...and a great percentage of the shanty dwellers don't want to work."

### *"What Kind of Future Can the [Lead-poisoned] Children Have?"*

"Rosario [Débora's grandmother] told me that the kids have lead. Lead makes you anemic, and you are prone to all sorts of illnesses. What kind of future can these children have? My brother lives a little bit farther away from the high-voltage wires. And he began to feel sick. He is younger than me. And I told him that he has to move out from here. But he says he doesn't have a place to go. Nobody would buy his house. In that block people are getting sick, the kind of sickness that not even doctors can figure out, they become languid, some lose their teeth, their hair..."

### *"Am I Scaring You, Débora?"*

Siri: See, after that gust of wind I smelled something strange. That's because I am now living elsewhere. I now notice. It was an awful smell....

Débora: Really? I didn't sense anything...

Siri: That's because it is slowly poisoning you. Sometimes when I come here, my eyes itch. That's because I come from a clean place. If you go somewhere else, when you come back you have to wear a mask, and you realize how bad it is to live in a place that is contaminated....

Débora: Now they say they are going to relocate us because of the pollution....

Siri: I think that's a good idea.... You are probably the same age of my daughter, right? How old are you? Twenty-eight, twenty-nine?

Débora: Twenty-seven...

Siri: It is important to do something before it is too late because then all sorts of incurable diseases accumulate, and your body doesn't have defenses.... After five years [of being here] you are poisoned. But it takes much longer to get cleaned. I know that for a fact because I worked in some really unhealthy places. I worked for two or three years and I won't be cured in less than twenty....

Débora: What happened to you?

Siri: I worked surrounded by dust. And I know that it hurt my bron-chus, my lungs, my eyes.... If you've been exposed to poison during three years, you need six or seven to be cleaned.... Am I scaring you, Débora? But it's the sad truth.

At the time of this interview, Siri's words did not scare Débora. But she did not ignore them. How could she? In point of fact, all the interviews, observations, informal conversations, and pictures we have been listening to, recording, and watching during the last two years had a certain "distancing" effect on her. While Javier was trying to get as close to Flammable residents as possible, Débora was slowly detaching herself from the place where she had lived since birth. At the same time she was learning to look at her environment as a social universe out of which a specific research object could be constructed (Bourdieu et al. 1991; Elias 2004). Gradually, and sometimes painfully, Débora was also rethinking some aspects of her life in Flammable and becoming aware of the possible effects that the contamination may have had on her. One of the outcomes of this difficult reflexive process was her decision to begin a series of clinical tests for damaging toxins. Siri's friendly advice ("It is important to do something before it's too late.... Am I scaring you?") then became a grim premonition of the things to come. In what follows we present some brief notes extracted from Débora's diary that document this reflexive process and then describe its (for both of us) unanticipated development.

## Débora's Life Notes

### September 27, 2005
Yesterday I graduated (anthropology). It's hard to learn what happens in the neighborhood through the photo-essay we did together with the schoolchildren. This research makes me face the reality here, what is really going on. I'd like this research to produce a book but not just that.

### October 7, 2005
After reading the articles that Javier sent me [referring to some papers on environmental health and social movements against pollution in the United States], many questions came back to my mind: With all I know now about the long-term effects of contamination, why am I still living here? Why don't I just get a job that provides me with enough money to move out of here? Sometimes I feel like dropping everything and moving to the countryside. But it is unfair: you have your own house, and you have to sell it and nobody would buy it. And ... I have roots here, all my family is here.

### November 3, 2005

I was ashamed of my neighborhood until my early twenties. I never wanted to bring friends here. Same thing with my boyfriends. And that might have been an impediment to some of my relationships. They always said it didn't matter, but I am not so sure that was actually the case.

### November 19, 2005

I talked with Olmos today, and he told me that he has "thick blood" and bad circulation. Karina also has "thick blood" and high blood pressure. Once I had a blood test done and they told me the same thing: that my blood was "thick." Could it be because of all the surrounding toxins? Every time I did an interview, and we talked about contamination, I ended up analyzing my own body. I looked at my own body through what my neighbors say about theirs . . . a denaturalization of the symptoms and of the possible effects of pollution.

### March 11, 2006

Sometimes I think that it is not that good for me to "get a change of air" and go on vacation to some other place. It is as if I decontaminate myself and then I come back to the same place. It is somewhat similar to what happens with the kids who begin the lead treatment and then return to the neighborhood.

### March 12, 2006

My stigma: sometimes I feel that people at work see me differently when they find out I live in Flammable: "poor kid . . . she is contaminated." It is as if they feel pity for me. It's something subtle. [It is as if] people scrutinize my skin, my body, as if they want to discover signs of contamination. . . . This makes me want to leave this place. I think I need to have some blood tests done. And then make enough money so that I can go and live somewhere else, so that I can at least not breathe this air.

Sometimes I think that no relocation is going to happen and that I should think about my own body and my own health first, and just leave. . . . The whole thing about the relocation is so difficult. But I need to think about myself and my own health. It may be in time to undo whatever the long-term exposure has done to me. But I also want to generate something in the neighborhood so that we can demand relocation.

*March 18, 2006*
I think it's a good idea to incorporate my "fieldnotes" into the book. What for anthropological work are simply "fieldnotes" for me are "life-notes." What for some colleagues are notes from the field, for me are notes on my own everyday life.

In these two years, Débora rediscovered her neighborhood and rediscovered herself or, better put, rediscovered herself through her inquiry into the neighborhood's history and present condition. She began to examine herself through a prism constructed by the images, the voices, and the sufferings of her neighbors. The more she heard about her neighbors' afflictions, the more she listened to them telling her stories about the past and present of Flammable, the more she read about the sources and effects of contamination, the more we discussed the contradictions inherent in the plethora of outside interventions, the more she thought about her own childhood and her own life in a different light. "Could I also be lead-poisoned?" she asked. "And who knows what other kinds of toxins I was exposed to? What long-term effects did that have?"

In these two years, as a product of reading and of endless, sometimes circular, conversations between us, Débora—we both now believe—came to denaturalize her own condition. It was not a linear process; and it was certainly a thorny one because once Débora slowly began to problematize her own body and health, she immediately began to think about the possible options: Should she leave? But what about her family? She began to seriously consider the possibility of moving out of the neighborhood, especially after a set of negative blood exams, but she also continually hesitated: Not only did she feel bad about leaving without her family but she also profoundly disliked the idea of an individual solution to a collective problem.

The whole process of self-discovery through ethnographic reflexivity gained momentum when Débora, during lunchtime at her house, told Javier about her anemia. Could it be related to lead? Or to her chronic exposure to above-average levels of benzene?[5] Débora consulted the doctors at the local health center. They told her that since she was a vegetarian, she should take some iron supplements and see what happens. Two months later, her red cells count went up again, and doctors told her that she should not worry about lead. And yet she insisted. Going against what we were learning about the widespread confusion and insecurity that dominate everyday life in Flammable, she wanted to have certainty; now her search was not about what was really going on the neighborhood but about what was really going on with her health. At Javier's insistence, Débora went to a private doctor and asked him to test her for heavy metals. The results showed 10 µg/dl, which is the upper limit of what dozens of studies consider a tolerable lead level. They also showed the presence of some indicators of other heavy chemicals in her bloodstream. She then decided to consult the doctors at the Hospital Fernandez, a very good state hospital that houses an important toxicological center.

When the doctors at Hospital Fernandez saw the test results, they told Débora that she should wash her clothes separately every time she comes back from the neighborhood. They also told her to avoid eating in Flammable. Once she clarified that she was not just working in the neighborhood but had lived there for twenty-seven years, they said matter-of-factly, "You have to leave." They also ordered further tests to check for "direct and indirect" indicators of poisoning. That night, Débora wrote: "As I was waiting in line at the hospital, and with the many lab orders in hand, quite overwhelmed, I couldn't help but thinking about those poor mothers in Flammable. I've been talking with them for the last two years. If the doctors prescribed them further tests, what do they do? They simply give up. . . . They can't afford them."

After consulting her clinical history, toxicologists at the Hospital Fernandez told her that her anemia might indeed be related to lead poisoning. They also educated her in many of the symptoms of lead deposits in bones (like slight trembles, mild abdominal pains, etc.) and told her to watch for them. "I am worried," she wrote in her notebook. "Even if a treatment 'decontaminates' me, even if I move out (as I plan to do) of Flammable, what are the long-term effects? Nobody seems to know. It is very hard to write this. Now, I don't really care about the book we are writing."

# Conclusion
## Ethnography and Environmental Suffering

A kind of rubbish that can never be got rid of, a poison that
will linger for all time, an everlasting blemish, permanent,
indomitable pandemonium.
—Françoise Zonabend

The best ethnographic study will never make the reader a
native....All that the historian or ethnographer can do, and all
that we can expect of them, is to enlarge a specific experience
to the dimensions of a more general one.
—Claude Levi-Strauss

Ana came to Villa Inflamable in 1995. With money provided by the local government and some compound companies, she organized a soup kitchen at
her house. She has a daughter and three sons—one of them, Eduardo, was
tested during the JICA study and is lead-poisoned. What follows is an (edited)
transcription of portions of a two-hour-long conversation we had with her in
March 2006. The dialogue touches on many of the most important themes of
our study: the first days in the neighborhood, the sick children, the rumors
about relocation, the role played by lawyers and doctors, and the impact that
the JICA study had in raising the issue of contamination among residents.

In Ana's conversation, assertions about contamination and its consequences are mixed with the hopes deposited on lawyers, the constant threat of
relocation, and the belief in the goodwill of the companies in the compound.
Ana's perspective does not summarize a "Flammable point of view" on the
subject of contamination; as we said, there is no such thing: no unique percep-
tual script exists. We chose her voice to end this book because, much like Siri
at the end of the last chapter, she in part agrees and in part disagrees with her
neighbors. It is this disagreement—together with Ana's doubts, her waiting,
and her confusion—that defines Flammable's toxic experience.

- *Filling with toxic waste*—"This [referring to her patio] was a small lagoon.
  We filled it with soil that trucks removed from there [pointing to the front

of her house] to make way for the street. It was all cement, stones, black
stuff. We paid 5 pesos per truck, and they put all the contents right here."

- *Lead-poisoned son*—"Eduardo is ashamed of going out with shorts
because of all the pimples. He has small scars all over him. Thank God,
he never had them on his face. I bought him long pants so that he can
cover the pimples. He doesn't sleep at night. It itches all over his back,
his arms, his legs. Manuel [her second son] is now getting rashes, too.
I am now waiting for the lawyers. They are coming to do some studies,
but I don't know what's going on because they haven't come yet. I call
them and they don't come."

- *Thinking (with others) about contamination*—"When they began
to recruit kids for the lead test [in 2001], I began thinking about his
pimples. . . . When they came and told me that he had lead I began to
think about contamination. The doctors here [at the local health center]
told me: 'No, mum, don't get scared. It's nothing.' . . . And now, I don't
know. It is as if nothing happened with the lead thing. No municipal
official came back. There were no more tests."

- *Waiting for the lawyer(s): "There is shit in the water. We have everything
on our side"*—"Before this one, we had some other lawyers . . . Doctor
Palacio and some others. They came, we signed [the power of attorney],
we had meetings, they explained stuff to us, and then, all of a sudden,
they disappeared. They were from the city. A neighbor brought them to
the neighborhood. I think it was through some local politician. They
never showed up again [in 2001]. We went to La Plata [the capital of the
state of Buenos Aires] to have blood tests done. We then got together
with a group of other mothers and we got another lawyer. His name
was Doctor Isla. We had meetings at my house, we signed papers, they
explained stuff to us. We came and went all over. They told us that we
could get money from the companies. Isla disappeared, he never came
back. One day, Doctor Russo came by. He came in November of last
year [2005]. Another day, he disappeared. But he came back. . . . This
one did return. I trust him. He stopped calling us during the last six
months . . . but he is very responsible. He had four families tested. But we
don't know the results. Apparently, he called one neighbor and told him
that the blood tests have to be done again. I don't know. It's been months
since he last came. I'm going to call him. . . . There is shit in the water, we
have everything on our side [to win the lawsuit] [El *agua tiene caca. Tenemos
todo a favor*]. The lawyer filed a lawsuit because we are unprotected here.

The lawyer told me: 'Ana, get ready, because you are going to have a good reward. We are about to win the lawsuit.' "

- *Relocation*—"We are going to be relocated, this year. Municipal officials say that by 2007 nobody should be living here. The owners of the land will pay us, they are going to give us a house. There are not going to be any more houses left here. This place is all going to be green space, and there will be industrial plants. All the companies, with the exception of Petrobras, put the money down [so that we can be relocated]. All the residents of Flammable are going to be removed.... But where are we going to go? They can't kick us out. If they give me 30,000 pesos [US $10,000], I'll move to Areco [in the province of Buenos Aires] with my cousin. It's pretty there.... But if they eradicate me, I don't know where am I going to go. What shall I do? I don't have a place to go. I don't know, I don't know."

- *The best company*—"To tell you the truth, we can't complain about Shell. It is the best company. It really supports us. And Tri Eco too. They give us milk and bread, 20 kilos of bread and 20 liters of milk. We can complain about the companies because whenever we need something, they provide.... [Shell PR director] Sieppe is very kind, very good."

"It is necessary," writes Pierre Bourdieu in *The Weight of the World*, "to learn to...give the marriage of a teacher and a post office worker the attention and interest that would have been given to the literary account of a misalliance, and to give the statements of a steelworker the thoughtful reception reserved by a certain tradition of reading for the highest forms of poetry or philosophy" (1999:624). To truly understand the experience of contamination, it is necessary, even imperative, to learn to listen to the seemingly anecdotal accounts of Flammable residents—to their statements concerning the smell of the now disappeared *quintas*, the size of the tomatoes and fruits harvested there, and the noise of the birds "back then," to their sometimes mistaken or illusory assertions as when they affirm: "I am not contaminated because I just had my blood tested, and it's all clear" or "Now, with this lawyer, we are going to nail the company down." And it is also important to dissect and scrutinize these assertions with the same, if not with more, analytical attention paid to the judgments of experts, be they lawyers, engineers, public health workers, or state officials. It is also crucial to examine—to bring to light and learn how to interpret and explain—the other "minor" details of everyday life in Flammable that ethnography is well equipped to detect: routine trips to the local health center and other hospitals made mostly by mothers with their sick children, occasional contacts made by neighbors with company personnel to ask for a specific favor, random appearances of reporters and lawyers in the neighborhood, rumors regarding imminent relocation, and meetings with this or that government official. Throughout this text, we focused attention on these words and deeds because, together, they are the substance of Flammable's toxic experience.

To present the reader with as luminous and thick a description of toxic experience as possible (Geertz 1973; Katz 2001, 2002), we resorted to traditional ethnographic fieldwork of the kind that still requires, as Mintz put it, "the same willingness to be uncomfortable, to drink bad booze, to be bored by one's drinking companions, and to be bitten by mosquitoes as always" (2000:170). We also focused our ethnographic attention on the actors and practices that have an influence on the ways in which locals think and feel about toxicity. The reader can label the result "multi-sited" or "shoe-leather" ethnography. We think of our fieldwork as an embedded and embodied form of inquiry that has kept constant vigilance over the outside determinants of the experience under scrutiny (on variants of fieldwork, see Burawoy 2000; Duneier 1999; Wacquant 2005). We moved *in and out* of Flammable to understand and explain the complex ways in which residents *make sense of their lives in the context of their daily routines, as opposed to making sense for an outsider.* We got close to our subjects but we also moved far from them, in order to better comprehend their views and actions. What did we learn specifically about Flammable and, more broadly, about environmental suffering in this back-and-forth process?

We have few doubts about the fact that, in postponing relocation, the state is perpetuating residents' toxic suffering, condemning a generation to live lead-loaded lives full of tragic consequences for their physical and mental health. We also have few doubts that the past and present uncontrolled emissions of compound companies make for a miserable life in this neighborhood-turned-industrial-zone. Now, the lived experience of suffering is not an exclusive product of unmonitored release of toxins. The ways in which residents make sense of their plight are permeated and determined by the many discursive and practical interventions that penetrate Flammable. In the experience of contamination, toxins matter, but so do noxious and puzzling words and actions, even those produced with the best intentions.

The manifold ways in which residents make sense of their fragile, vulnerable condition is hard to understand and explain without looking, simultaneously, at what other actors do toward and say about them. Examined from this social-constructivist perspective, statements such as "We have shit in the water. We have everything on our side" make perfect sense. In the midst of pollutants' assault and of widespread confusion and uncertainty regarding their source and effects, many residents believe that their suffering—their kids' rashes and allergies, their own headaches and general feeling of exhaustion—has a meaning. From their points of view, theirs is not a "useless suffering" (Levinas 1998) but one that, in the hands of a good lawyer or an ambitious reporter, can be put to good use. Their suffering has a meaning, and their waiting makes sense: they have "everything on their side."

Lawyers' deeds and words are now part of residents' schemes of perception and evaluation. And so are those of government officials and local physicians: Flammable residents' perceptions and feelings about lead, for example, are hard to imagine apart from the epidemiological study supported by the local government. Ana's words are quite clear on this. She began thinking about her son's pimples in a different way after the lead study began. Her doubts, furthermore, should be situated in the context of the reassuring words of doctors (or, better, in the context of what she *understands* doctors are telling her): "I don't know. It is as if nothing happened with the lead thing." These uncertainties are compounded by the always-present threat of eviction—relocation that is said to be carried out mainly because of the presence of dangerous pollutants in the area.[1] The language and the actions of compound companies are also part of neighbors' frames. In an instructive example of the operation of symbolic violence, whereby the dominated shared the categories of perception with the dominant (Bourdieu 1991; Bourdieu and Wacquant 1992), we see many residents thinking of the compound's more prominent firms as the "best companies" and as "good providers." Would it be too far-fetched to argue that these views and (in)actions support residents' own domination?

The relationship between objective (contaminated) space and subjective (toxic) representations (or between habitat and habitus) is thus a complex one. Residents are, indeed, disposed because they are exposed (Bourdieu 2000:140), but the set of confused, contradictory, and mistaken understandings, or *mis-cognitions*, to borrow Bourdieu's word, engendered by long-term exposure to pollutants is mediated by the many appropriations, denials, and distortions carried out by existing institutions. These uses and misuses of contamination mold the ways in which residents see, judge, and individually or collectively act or fail to act upon their conditions of existence. These actions, views, and appraisals, in turn, support their own powerlessness and perpetuate their toxic exposure.

What we witness in Flammable is thus a specific variation of the general experience of domination. Flammable illustrates not only what living in toxic danger is all about but also, more generally, how domination works and how it is lived.

Our task as ethnographers has been to emphasize the particularities of this case while, at the same time, examining how this distinctiveness relates to general discussions about the links between suffering and powerlessness and about the social production of uncertainty. Paraphrasing Levi-Strauss, we sought to enlarge Flammable's specific toxic experience to the dimensions of a more general one.

We are deeply aware of the moral and political dilemmas revolving around attempts to represent the suffering and the domination of others. In a book that discusses the diverse appropriations and transformations of the torment of Flammable residents carried out by all sorts of professionals and state officials, we would be blind not to notice that our scholarly dissection and presentation of residents' afflictions is also a form of appropriation, or, in the words of Veena Das, a "professional transformation of suffering" (1995:143). We took the risk of researching on, and writing about, Flammable residents' plight because we are concerned about the dangers of mimicking society's silence toward this same suffering (Das 1997). Although the link between environment and health is slowly emerging as a topic of public interest in contemporary Argentina, the highly unequal distribution of hazards and the suffering of those at the losing end of this distribution are routinely displaced as a nonurgent theme. As an exercise in public social science, this book's broader aim has been to help readers to acknowledge environmental suffering as a topic of pressing concern—a topic that, despite much research on inequality and poverty in Latin America, has remained quite marginal. This marginality, in turn, reflects the secondary status of environmental concerns among policy-makers and government officials.[2] If we step back from this specific social universe and take a larger, structural view, we might say that what we witness in Flammable is durable inequality in the making: an inequality that is being created not by wage inequity (which has been exhaustively studied; see Tilly 1998) but by the relationship between environment and health, which, although crucial to the well-being of the population, has been traditionally neglected in studies of Latin America's persistent inequality.

One larger implication for social science research thus emerges from this case study. Any sociological sketch of urban marginality should pay sustained and systematic empirical attention to the contaminated or hazardous environment where the urban poor dwell. It is crucial to put environmental justice at the center of analyses of poverty in Latin America. Together with income, employment, education, and the other conventional variables, analyses of the causes and manifestations of urban deprivation should take account of poor people's differential exposure to environmental hazards. Marginality is, to paraphrase geographer Doreen Massey (1994), constructed spatially—and that space is burdened with pollution and other risks. This spatial organization of marginality makes a difference in how it works and how it is experienced. Because living in constant danger and under unrelenting toxic assault leaves sometimes indelible marks on the minds and bodies of the poor, urban research in Latin American urgently needs a social geography of environmental danger and suffering.[3]

Throughout this book, we have presented many individual testimonies that speak about suffering. The experiences of affliction, however, are not simply individual. They are social because, although located in individual bodies and expressed in individual voices, they are actively created by the position that Flammable residents as a group occupy as materially and symbolically deprived persons, both in the broader social macrocosmos and in the specific social microcosmos of a highly contaminated neighborhood.

The experiences of suffering are social in a second sense as well: the meanings attributed by residents to their condition depend on specific situations, relational settings, and available cultural representations. This book has documented the many different ways of "living toxicity" and has centered on confusion and uncertainty as prevailing themes in the shared experiences of suffering. One of the substantive lessons we learned along the way is that toxic representations and experiences are incomprehensible without bringing in the broader material and symbolic context: Flammable's historic relationship with the compound and the plethora of outside interventions. The source of what people live in Flammable lies outside its territorial boundaries—not only do toxins invade the neighborhood, so do words and actions. We paid sustained attention to these discourses and these concrete actions because they are an important part of the material and symbolic order in Flammable; words and actions by outside agents give form to the ways residents think and feel about their lives and their surroundings. In other words, our analysis confirms and expands Bourdieu's analysis of site effects: "The essential principle of what is lived and seen on the ground—the most striking testimony and the most dramatic experience—is elsewhere" (Bourdieu et al. 1999:123).

A larger analytical lesson is then the following: The study of environmental suffering is—together with a dissection of the "hard facts" of pollution—a study of the experiences and the meanings attributed to this suffering. An ethnography of environmental suffering is a study of the voices of the sufferers but also a study of the narratives whirling around the lives of the residents—of all the attempts to make sense of this suffering; of all the public acknowledgments and appropriations, which are, as the analysis of this book implies, deeply political acts (Todeschini 2001).

There is also a methodological lesson to be learned from our analysis. We came close, usually very close, to our subjects but avoided parroting their views by linking them to the system of material and symbolic relations (encapsulated in terms such as "organic relationship" and "labor of confusion") that related the neighborhood to its larger context. We focused attention on the relationship between the lived meanings of toxicity and the social construction of confusion and uncertainty not because we encountered this topic ready-made while conducting fieldwork as the I-began-to-get-ideas-in-the-field approaches to ethnography would have it (Wacquant 2002:1481), but because we were, first and foremost, interested in the linkages between collective suffering and power relations (Arendt 1973; Kleinman, Das, and Lock 1997). Data collection in this sense should be properly termed data production in that it was intimately bound with the theoretical construction of the ethnographic object (Bourdieu et al. 1991; Wacquant 2002).[4]

Now, this is more easily said than done, especially when the research is a joint venture between persons who not only come from different disciplines but, more important, are located in different positions in the social and academic space (Débora, a resident of Flammable with a recent bachelor's degree in anthropology, and Javier, a tenured sociologist living in the United States) and who have, accordingly, diverse sets of interests (one more activistic, the other one more scholarly). We will avoid turning this last page into a narcissistic reflection on joint research and coauthorship. The proof of the virtues and pitfalls of this sort of collaboration is, after all, the book that the reader is about to finish. Let us simply state that this book represents a transitory point of contact in the lives of a local, "native," anthropologist and a somewhat foreign sociologist. We brought two disciplines and two standpoints together to produce what we take to be a quite revealing understanding and explanation of collective suffering amid toxic assault. Although we will probably continue along separate trajectories, we find in ethnographic fieldwork and writing a common ground. Many different individual, academic, and political reasons entered into our joint decision to write a book about Flammable. And those reasons kept changing as we progressed in our fieldwork, as we came to know residents better and as our perceptions of our own selves changed—in the case of Débora, the "native," in quite a radical way. But there was one reason, one motivating force, call it a *scholarly and political libido* if you will, that we both shared from the very beginning of this adventure: This book was conceived of as our way of telling Flammable residents that we are concerned with them, we are with them, we are listening to their stories, and we will testify to what they are living through. If anything, this book bears witness to their experiences of toxic suffering.

# Acknowledgments

This book would not have been possible without the collaboration of the residents of Villa Inflamable. To preserve their anonymity, we have changed some of their names. Each of them knows how much we appreciate their help, though some may disagree with parts of our analysis. We here wish to reiterate to them that our work was carried out with our best intentions: We wrote this book out of sheer indignation about what we witnessed and heard in order to spread the word about living conditions in the neighborhood and the plight of its inhabitants. We honestly hope that this book will trigger a debate, inside and outside the neighborhood (a shorter version is being published simultaneously in Spanish), that will cast them as its main players and that will lead to real solutions to the problems they face.

More than three years ago, Máximo Lanzetta put us in touch; out of that first meeting we began the collaboration that led to this book. Máximo shared with us all his vast knowledge about environmental matters and his policy-making experience. Although he is not responsible for what we say here (and he might also disagree with parts of our analysis) it is fair to say that, without him, there would not have been collaborative research and book. *Gracias Máximo!*

We presented parts of this book at the Practicing Pierre Bourdieu conference at the University of Michigan; at the Ethnografeast III in Lisbon, Portugal; at the conference "On Community and the Poor in Latin America" at Northwestern University; at the anthropology department at the Universidad Autónoma Metropolitana-Itztapalapa, Mexico City; at the sociology department at the University of Texas–Austin; and at the centers of Latin American studies at the University of Pittsburgh and at Syracuse University. A first draft of chapters 2 and 3 was presented at the sociology department at the State University of New York at Stony Brook. We wish to thank participants at these diverse fora for their critical feedback. We are also grateful to those who read parts of the manuscript: Ciska Raventos, Luis Reygadas, Lucas Rubinich, Rosalía Winocur, Brodie Fischer, Gabriela Merlinsky, Michael Schwartz, Gilda Zwerman, Louis Esparza, Gene Lebowicz, María Epele, and Loïc Wacquant. Naomi Rosenthal deserves a special place in this acknowledgment: she read (and reread) various chapters and provided many substantive and stylistic comments. Thanks also to Lauren Joseph, who carefully edited the manuscript and who helped Javier with the management of the journal *Qualitative Sociology* while he was immersed in the writing of this book. Much of the merit for the well-oiled working of the journal (and its expansion!) belongs to her. Preliminary versions of chapters 2, 3 and 5 were published in the journals *American Sociological Review*, *Sociological Forum*, *Contexts*, and *Ethnography*; we wish to thank these journals' editors and our anonymous reviewers for their comments on form and content. At the Lisbon Ethnografeast,

Philippe Bourgois suggested a relationship between our formal account of the social production of uncertainty presented in chapter 7 and the workings of symbolic violence. We are very grateful for that comment, which shaped much of what we wrote in chapter 7 and in the conclusion. Similarly, we wish to acknowledge Eileen Otis, who read versions of chapters 4 and 7 and provided insightful and detailed comments, particularly regarding the relationship between the "temporal dispersion" of contamination (the phrase is actually hers) and residents' categories of perception. And thanks to Matthew Mahler, whose detection of a relationship between our understanding of "toxic confusion" and Willis's concept of "partial penetrations" motivated us to rethink part of our argument. Javier wishes to acknowledge the financial support of the American Council of Learned Societies. An ACLS fellowship provided funding to finish the fieldwork and to complete this manuscript.

We thank the doctoral students of Javier's seminar "Social Suffering: Causes and Experiences" at the sociology department of the State University of New York–Stony Brook for critical observations that helped to improve the final manuscript. Thanks to Amy Braksmajer, Aura Caplett, Misty Currelli, Elizabeth Doswell, Hernan Sorgentini, Amy Dunkel, Rachel Kalish, Gabriel Hernandez, Can Ersoy, Fernanda Page and Deidre Caputo-Levine. Pablo Lapegna took the seminar and deserves a special acknowledgment; our common interests and many conversations about "environmental suffering" were a crucial contribution to this book.

Débora wishes to extend special thanks to her neighbors, who opened not only the doors of their homes but also, and most important, their hearts, sharing with her their hopes, frustrations, and dreams. She is also grateful to those who heard part of the story we tell in the book (and by extension her own story) and who helped her to achieve the hard-to-obtain "epistemological distance": Paula Estrella, Eugenia Dejo, Carolina Maidana, Rodrigo Hobert, Susana Ortale, and most of all, her coauthor. She is also thankful to those who commented on a draft of chapter 3 at the IV Jornadas de Investigación en Antropología Social at the Instituto de Ciencias Antropológicas of the Universidad de Buenos Aires and at the FLACSO-Ecuador International Congress.

Essential also were the moments of fun she shared with Anita Forlano, Celeste Isasmendi, Marina Flores, Ana Gutierrez and Alejandra Carreras; and the delicious lunches with her mother, Elsa, in the midst of "fieldwork." Débora also wants to extend a big thanks to her family who is always there, with and for her, and who constitute the main reason for her to embark in the task of researching (and writing about) her neighborhood. *Gracias a todos!*

We were extremely fortunate to have James Cook and Christine Dahlin as our editors at Oxford University Press; our thanks to both of them for their initial faith on this project, their enthusiastic support throughout, and their detailed editorial work.

In September 2004, as the project was slowly taking shape, Javier showed Chuck Tilly an aerial picture of Flammable. From the very beginning, Chuck was complicit in this book. Looking attentively at the picture that shows the shantytown threatened by all sort of hazards, he heard Javier doubt out loud about the possible ways of studying "toxic suffering," discussed with him alternative plans for the research, and provided his guidance. He even suggested a title for this book ("Living in Danger"). Though we did not heed that particular bit of advice, his other comments were a crucial help at an early stage of this project (in fact, his "Invisible Elbow" inspired much of the analysis of the connections between relations, routines, and uncertainty). He then read two drafts of this manuscript and gave us his illuminating suggestions for revision. Chuck's immense generosity, curiosity, humility, openness, and sagacity will be missed dearly. He was a brilliant intellectual and scholar, a unique advisor with an unparalleled kindness and egalitarianism—a noble man who was always there for us, offering an insightful conversation, a penetrating remark in a workshop, an encouraging e-mail in response to a query, a reaction to a paper that always came sooner than expected. This book is dedicated to his memory.

# Notes

## Introduction

1. Most names in the text, with the exception of public officials, Shell officials, and some community leaders and/or activists, have been changed to ensure anonymity.

2. We wish to thank Philippe Bourgois for making us aware of the fact that we are opening up the "symbolic violence box" and looking at its main components and relations.

3. For a recent review of research on and protest against "environmental racism," see Pellow (2005); for discussions on environmental inequality see Anderton et al. (1994); Krieg (1998); Gould (1998); Weinberg (1998); Mitchell, Thomas, and Cutter (1999); Davidson and Anderton (2000); and Downey (2005).

4. For an illuminating application of cognitive heuristics to the study of policy diffusion, see Weyland (2005). For an illustration of the working of heuristics for the case of toxic poisoning, see Heimer's (1988) interpretation of Clarke (1989) and Levine (1982).

5. For work emphasizing ambiguities in understandings of risk and contradictions in official discourse, see Françoise Zonabend's (1993) study of risk perceptions among residents living near a nuclear reprocessing plant in Normandy, France. Studies by MacGill (1989) and by Reilly (1999) provide a plethora of evidence regarding the variety of meanings that people attach to risk in their daily lives—and particularly, the "depth, complexity and ambiguity" of people's "risk attitudes" (MacGill 1989:62)—and the factors that shape them. Similar in analytical intent, our study differs with the two aforementioned in the kind of specification we provide regarding the sources of collective "risk frames" and in the substantive conclusions we reached. Unlike MacGill and Reilly, we detected neither a *decreasing reliance* on expert systems when it comes to assess risks (or, in the words of Reilly [1999:137], a "re-evaluation both of the media as a source of critical information and of politicians/government officials as reliable providers of health messages") nor an *increasing reflexivity* in residents' monitoring of toxic risks (in the words of Reilly [1999: 144], the adjustment of "beliefs and practices in light of new information"). For a summary of these two studies and their relationship to Beck's "risk society" approach, see Myhen (2004).

6. Another (in this case, technological) disaster serves to illustrate the point. In her insightful study of the aftermath of the Chernobyl nuclear catastrophe, Adriana Petryna (2002) dissects in all their complexity the manifold interventions that mediated between the actual event and the knowledge and practices that ensued. As she puts it:

> The physical reality of the Chernobyl disaster and its sheer magnitude were
> initially refashioned and refracted through a series of informational omissions,
> technical strategies, errors, semiempirical models, approximations, international

cooperations, and limited interventions. Combined, these practices initially produced a picture of a known, circumscribed, and manageable biological reality. Later, these biological effects were seen as political products; technical unknowns were reshaped in the subsequent Ukrainian period as part of a new biopolitical regime. Informal economies of knowledge, codified symptoms, differential medical access, a continuum of diagnoses, and 'Chernobyl ties' were mobilized and began to function as institutions in parallel with the state's official, legal social protection system. (216)

For the case of Flammable, the implications of Petryna's work are clear: the knowledge (and ignorance) of industrial pollution and its attendant health effects are always socially and politically constructed and contested ("refashioned and refracted") by all sorts of actors—in the case at hand, victims, state authorities, doctors, lawyers, and other interested parties.

7. As Phillimore et al. (2000) write:

It is in the nature of epidemiological research design that there will always be pieces missing from the jigsaw, unrecognized or underestimated confounding factors or biases. Some of these inherent problems are sharply thrown into relief if we consider one relevant factor: time. The concept of the "long term" is relevant in three senses here, each of which makes judgments about health effects harder: *the long duration of most exposures to pollution, the longtime lag between cumulative exposure and medical symptoms; and the chronic nature of ill-health once symptoms manifest themselves.* These long time frames quite reasonably militate against confident claims about causation in epidemiological studies, and help to ensure that such claims are more than usually hedged around with caution and qualification.... *Caution may swiftly be interpreted as inconclusiveness for political reasons.* (230, our emphasis)

8. On "native anthropology," see Ohnuki-Tierney (1984) and Narayan (1993).

9. As noted in a previous work (Auyero 2007), Javier heard about Cubist ethnography from sociologist Jack Katz. Much of the inspiration for the combination of narrative strategies comes from Loïc Wacquant's book *Body and Soul.* On interdisciplinary collaboration in the study of social suffering, see Bourdieu et al. (1999) and Kleinman, Das, and Lock (1997).

10. For examinations of the links between environment and inequality, see the numerous studies on "environmental justice" and "environmental racism." This scholarship has long noticed the manifold ways in which race and class shape the health and environments of communities of color in the United States. For some illustrative examples, see Bullard (1990, 1993, 2005); Cole and Foster (2001); and Pellow (2002). For a recent review of the anthropological literature on the subject, see Nguyen and Peschard (2003); for a recent overview of the public health literature, see Evans and Kantrowitz (2002); for a comprehensive compilation of sociological and historical studies on the impact of the environment on health, see Kroll-Smith, Brown, and Gunter (2000). For illustrative and moving "tales" about the pernicious effects of pollution on health, see D. Davis (2002).

11. The same omission does not hold true for the case of the rural poor, see Angus Wright's classic *The Death of Ramón González: The Modern Agricultural Dilemma*, where he documents many cases of pesticide poisoning among migrant farm workers.

## Chapter 1

1. María Cristina Cravino's (2006) recent comprehensive study constitutes the only real exception to this general absence of factual knowledge about the state of the shantytowns of Buenos Aires.

2. For UN-habitat researchers, the term "slum" encompasses shanties, squatter settlements, and other types of informal housing.

3. Greater Buenos Aires comprises the twenty-four districts that surround the city of Buenos Aires, also known as *Conurbano*. According to a study conducted by geographers at the Universidad de General Sarmiento (*La Nación*, July 10, 2006), 638,657 people lived in 385 precarious settlements in 2001, and about 1,144,500 lived in a thousand precarious settlements in 2006.

4. On the policies of the government of the state and the city of Buenos Aires toward shantytowns and squatter settlements, see Cravino (2006, 2007a).

5. This process is described in detail in Auyero (2001).

6. This quotation is from a story that appeared in the newspaper *La Nación* on September 27, 2004, which also reported the reemergence of tuberculosis and leprosy in the shantytowns of Buenos Aires. On April 26, 2006, responding to a report by local ombudsman that described the collapse of the sewer and water systems serving the shantytowns located in Bajo Flores, Soldati, Lugano and Mataderos, the government of the city of Buenos Aires declared them "zones of sanitary risk."

7. Investigative reporter Robert Neuwirth (2005:5) also notes what appears to be a defining feature of many a slum in Buenos Aires: life here takes place amid industrial and human waste. Describing the setting in Southland, a shanty community on the western side of Nairobi, Kenya, he writes:

A mound of garbage formed the border between Southland and the adjacent legal neighborhood of Langata. It was perhaps 8 feet tall, 40 feet long, and 10 feet wide, set in a wider watery ooze. As we passed, two boys were climbing the Mt. Kenya of trash. They couldn't have been more than 5 or 6 years old. They were barefoot, and with each step their toes sank into the muck, sending hundreds of flies scattering from the rancid pile. I thought they might be playing King of the Hill. But I was wrong. Once atop the pile, one of the boys lowered his shorts, squatted, and defecated. The flies buzzed hungrily around his legs.

8. On the state and fate of the *Riachuelo*, see the detailed report produced by the Federal Ombudsman Office (Defensoría del Pueblo de la Nación Argentina, 2003). See also Merlinsky (2007b).

9. For a full description of living conditions in Villa Jardín, see Auyero (2001).

10. For a brief vivid chronicle of life on the banks of the Riachuelo, see Alarcón (2006). For a cultural history of the river's landscape, see Silvestri (2004).

### Chapter 2

1. www.shell.com.ar.

2. The local improvement association is still called Sociedad de fomento pro mejoramiento de la costa.

3. We asked thirteen ninth-grade students of the local school to divide themselves into groups (five groups of two students each and one of three students) and we gave them disposable cameras containing twenty-seven exposures each. They were told to use half the film to take pictures of things they liked about the neighborhood and half on things they did not like. We gave them no further instructions. They all returned the cameras providing a total number of 134 pictures. We then selected the pictures that better represent the themes that were recurrent in the whole group.

4. "The factories release a lot of smoke," Manuela tells us. "It's all full of oil. I didn't take a picture (of the smokestacks) because the sun was in front of me."

5. Though technically outside the petrochemical compound, the incinerator of hazardous waste (Trieco) was also mentioned as a source of pollution: "People say that at night, they burn things at Trieco, and it's very, very ugly" (Romina).

6. The youngsters we interviewed have a view on their surroundings that is more uniform than that of the adults for two reasons: (1) they use the public space of the neighborhood (streets, plazas, open fields) much more frequently than do adults; and (b) many of their teachers (who do not live in the neighborhood) have a homogenous view on contamination and its sources, and they communicate it to their students. As we were told by two school principals and two teachers in almost identical way: "This place is all contaminated because of Shell. Contamination is killing the kids." Their homogenous view might also have been the outcome of the conditions under which our interviews with them were carried out. These interviews were closer to one-time encounters than to the kind of conversations, based on long term acquaintance, that we had with adults—we met with them three times: when we presented the photography project, when we gave them the cameras and minimal instructions, and when we reviewed their pictures and interviewed them. Alas, these students may have seen us as "outsiders," with the biased results that we described in the beginning of chapter 4.

7. The unemployment subsidy known as Plan Jefas y Jefes (see the introduction) and state-funded soup kitchens are the two main state programs serving Flammable residents.

8. Mate is a beverage that is very popular in Argentina, Paraguay, Uruguay, and southern Brazil. It's made from steeping the leaves of the mate bush in hot water.

9. The other companies within the compound had a more erratic relationship with the neighborhood. Decades ago, for example, the Compañía General de Combustibles (later Eg3 and now Petrobrás) donated pipes to bring potable water into the neighbor-

hood. Other companies also made donations to the local improvement association. None, however, achieved the kind of regular relationship that Shell had and still has with the barrio.

10. Starting in the 1930s, industrialization in Buenos Aires fueled migration from the provinces (Rock 1987; Torrado 2004).

11. A list of the activities the company funds (and the goods it distributes) throughout Avellaneda can be found at www.shell.com.ar.

12. As we were revising this manuscript for publication, we learned that the federal Department of Environmental Policy and Sustainable Development decided to temporarily close the Shell refinery. Among other things, the department mentioned "contamination" of the surrounding grounds as an argument for the closing. The refinery was reopened four days later (see Clarín.com, September 6 to 9, 2007).

13. On the clandestine garbage dumps in Buenos Aires, see Defensoría del Pueblo de la Nación Argentina (2003: 195–210).

14. Chromium is a known carcinogen that is listed as a "hazardous air pollutant" by the U.S. Environmental Protection Agency.

15. According to the EPA:
The central nervous system (CNS) is the primary target organ for toluene toxicity in both humans and animals for acute (short-term) and chronic (long-term) exposures. CNS dysfunction and narcosis have been frequently observed in humans acutely exposed to toluene by inhalation; symptoms include fatigue, sleepiness, headaches, and nausea.... Chronic inhalation exposure of humans to toluene also causes irritation of the upper respiratory tract and eyes, sore throat, dizziness, and headache. Human studies have reported developmental effects, such as CNS dysfunction, attention deficits, and minor craniofacial and limb anomalies, in the children of pregnant women exposed to toluene or mixed solvents by inhalation.... EPA has classified toluene as a Group D, not classifiable as to human carcinogenicity. (http://www.epa.gov/ttn/atw/hlthef/toluene.html)

16. Ten micrograms per deciliter ($\mu$g/dl) is now considered to be a normal blood level of lead. On this history of lead epidemiology, see Berney (2000) and Widener (2000). On the history of "deceit and denial" concerning the pernicious effects of lead, see Markowitz and Rosner (2002). See also Warren (2000).

17. Exposure to environmental toxins such as lead has been examined as one of those early life conditions that have far-reaching consequences in adult life (and death). The long-term effects of lead-poisoning illustrate one facet of what demographers Mark Hayward and Bridget Gorman dub "the long arm of childhood": the influence of early-life conditions on mortality.

18. In a 2001 report, Greenpeace calls Tri Eco a "cancer factory" and details the lack of state controls over it. Tri Eco burns, among other things, the pathogenic residues of approximately seventeen public hospitals. That same report asserts that Tri Eco is also contaminating soil and water streams with lead.

19. As Zonabend (1993:53) asserts about residents living near a nuclear waste processing plant in Normandy, they "have been convinced that what happens at the plant is kept from them, or at least that they will learn of it only in roundabout ways. They feel that, whatever they do, they are excluded from and have no control over the sources of information and knowledge."

20. Curiously enough, African-American residents in Diamond, Louisiana, tell similar stories about the relocation of original inhabitants forced by Shell; see Lerner (2005).

21. *Fieldnote (Débora), January 9, 2006*: "Between 7.43 and 7.53 A.M. I counted eight trucks making their way through Sargento Ponce Street (the street that goes into Petrobras refinery). At 8 P.M. there are thirty trucks parked in Shell's lot, right in front of Shell's gate. Those go through Larroque, not through my street." The houses in Danubio are located very close to the street that goes to the Petrobras refinery, and the constant truck traffic makes them tremble during the peak hours [see Photo 5.1]. Accidents provoked by the heavy traffic are quite common. On February 27, 2006, a twelve-year-old girl was killed by an oil truck while she was riding her bicycle.

## Chapter 3

1. The air-quality monitoring is known as JICA I; the epidemiological study is known as JICA II.

2. In a meeting with a reporter from *Página12* (in which Axel Garde was present) the general manager of the refinery, Blas Vinci, asserted: "In the last decade, Shell invested US $250 million in the areas of safety and environment." Top managers from Shell assured the reporter that everything "was under control, that there are no leaks, and that the risks of accident are fantasies" (*Página12*, June 23, 2002).

3. On the relationship between blood lead levels and leaded gasoline, see Thomas (1995). For a case study of the health effects of an oil refinery in a nearby community, see Lerner (2005).

4. www.epa.gov.

5. www.epa.gov/lead.

6. Personal communication with Máximo Lanzetta, current undersecretary of environmental policy in the state of Buenos Aires, October 21, 2005.

7. In their analysis of the relationship between uncertainty, contamination and politics in Teesside (North-East England), Phillimore et al. (2000) note a similar process. After remarking that "when the activities of major corporations are implicated" (217) environmental epidemiology is quite contentious, they describe the ways in which industry (and government) in Teesside "cast doubt about any plausible link between industrial air pollution and mortality" (224). From the dominant's point of view, poverty is the main cause of affliction. As the authors write (our emphasis): "Poverty has proved to be a less contentious issue than pollution in Teesside politics. *By magnifying the well-recognized links between unemployment or poverty and health as an explanation of unequal health patterns, any role of pollution in this equation is effectively weakened.*"

8. On "organizational deceit" as a powerful source of enmity and discord in environmental health, see Brown et al (2000), and Clarke's (1989) classic study on PCB contamination in Binghamton.

9. For an analogous process of "transformation and appropriation" of suffering, see Das' (1995) analysis of the Bhopal industrial disaster.

## Chapter 4

1. A few months after this conversation took place, Antonio, Débora's grandfather, died.

2. For a recent exception, see Wolford's (2006) illuminating analysis of "common sense" among Brazilian peasants involved with the MST (Movement of Rural Landless Workers). See also many of the essays in Pierre Bourdieu et al.'s *The Weight of the World*.

3. See also the Greenpeace report (2001).

4. The dozens of testimonies by old-timers belie Shell's assertion ("no responsible company dumped anything outside the compound's premises"): almost every other neighbor remembers the trucks coming out from the compound discharging *vaya uno a saber qué* (who knows what) in Flammable.

5. The Comité de Control y Monitoreo Ambiental held twenty meetings between January 2002 and August 2003. We had access to the minutes of those meetings thanks to a public official who attended them.

6. In May and December of that year, Greenpeace organized two protests in the area. In the first one, on May 22, Greenpeace activists blocked the entrance to Tri-Eco saying it was a "cancer factory." In the second, on the anniversary of the Bhopal industrial disaster, Greenpeace activists placed eight hundred white crosses in an open field in front of the compound protesting the lack of state policies to control toxic emissions in the area.

7. Avellaneda's undersecretary of health said so in a popular TV program (*La Liga*, June 2006), which included interviews with Flammable residents. He asserted: "The solution to the problem of contamination is the straightforward eradication [*la erradicación lisa y llana*] of the petrochemical compound."

8. On physicians' failures to deal with environmental hazards in the United States, see Brown and Kelley (2000).

## Chapter 5

1. We borrow the term "tempography" from Eviatar Zerubavel (1979) who in turn borrows it from Murray Melbin's essay "The Colonization of Time."

2. According to the U.S. National Institute of Neurological Disorders and Stroke, Arnold Chiari malformation is "a condition in which the cerebellum portion of the brain protrudes into the spinal canal." Gonzalo has the Arnold-Chiari type II malformation "associated with myelomeningocele (a defect of the spine) and hydrocephalus (increased cerebrospinal fluid and pressure within the brain), which usually are apparent at birth. Myelomeningocele usually causes paralysis of the legs and, less commonly, the arms. If

left untreated, hydrocephalus can cause mental impairment. Either type of Arnold-Chiari Malformation can cause symptoms of headache, vomiting, difficulty swallowing, and hoarseness. . . . Infants with very severe malformations may have life-threatening complications." Verónica knows that surgery might reduce Gonzalo's symptoms, but she is scared to have it done. "Maybe he'll have the surgery when he is older," she says. http://www.ninds.nih.gov/disorders/chiari/chiari.htm.

3. Fieldnote (Débora), February 10, 2006: "The container was stolen. Some people say that the municipality took it. My cousin saw a truck with the logo of the municipality taking the container. People keep throwing the garbage there. And the grocery owner burns it every two days. But the dogs ripped the trash bags, and there's garbage all over. Sometimes it's really awful. We called the municipality but nothing happened."

4. In another conversation, Verónica told us that she was pregnant (with Gonzalo) while working as a cleaner in one of the plants. One day, "I accidentally spilled some container with chemicals, the odor was terrible, and I fainted. They took me to the hospital, and they fired me the following week." At least twice in our conversations she wondered out loud about the possibility that this episode could have produced Gonzalo's Arnold Chiari disease.

## Chapter 6

1. For a classic statement on collective inaction and the power mechanisms involved in producing it, see Gaventa (1980).

2. See interview with one of the lawyers of the "mega-causa," Santiago Kaplun, in www.lavaca.org. The report is titled "The Rebellion of the Contaminated."

3. Road blockade is a form of protest that became quite generalized throughout Argentina in the last decade (Auyero 2002).

4. On collective action repertoires, see Tilly (1986, 2006); on collective discursive repertoires, see Steinberg (1999).

5. On the variable nature of grievances as an important factor in mobilization, see Walsh (1981). We thank Mayer Zald for making us aware of this crucial point.

6. See http://www.pagina12.com.ar/diario/dialogos/index-2006–07–24.html.

## Chapter 7

1. For a call for similar ethnographic studies in naturalistic settings, see Vaughan (1998).

2. On routines as attention-shaping and thought-structuring processes, see Heimer (2001).

3. On the containment of risk through the performance of everyday activities, see Skinner (2000).

4. For a description of these different practices, see Cerulo (2006), especially chapter 3.

5. Benzene and lead are both associated with low red-cell count and thus with anemia.

## Conclusion

1. As we write this, new talks of relocation have reemerged (backed by a Supreme Court decision demanding the clean-up of the Riachuelo and its adjacent areas), and some companies were ordered to move out of the compound because of their contaminating effects. Approximately twenty-five families (Karina Olmos's included) were assigned new homes in nearby Wilde. Karina's oldest son and his girlfriend decided to stay in Flammable—at Karina's house. Even if massive relocation occurs, neighbors will probably never know what effects their sustained exposure to toxins has had on their bodies.

2. On the role of writers as cultural producers who "can expand the borders of the moral community and force us to acknowledge suffering where we normally do not see it," see Morris (1997).

3. Given that many times we find out about hazards and its attendant health effects from collective actions triggered by them, this geography of environmental danger and suffering should also be a study of the spatial distribution of the popular contention organized around ecological threats.

4. As Wacquant (following Pierre Bourdieu) argues (2002:1523) in his scathing critique of the pitfalls of U.S. urban ethnography, we need to "recognize that there is not such a thing as ethnography that is not guided by theory (albeit vague and lay) and to draw the implications, that is, to work self-consciously to integrate them actively at every step in the construction of the object rather than to pretend to discover theory 'grounded' in the field, import it wholesale postbellum, or to borrow it ready-made in the form of clichés from policy debates."

# References

Abu-Lughod, Lila. 2000. "Locating Ethnography." *Ethnography* 1(2): 261–67.

Alarcón, Cristian. 2006. "Vivir junto al Riachuelo." *Página12*, May 23.

———. 2003. *Cuando me muera quiero que me toquen cumbia: Vidas de pibes chorros.* Buenos Aires: Norma.

Altimir, Oscar, Luis Beccaria, and Martín Gonzales Rozada. 2002. "Income Distribution in Argentina 1974–2002." *Cepal Review* 78.

Anderton, Douglas; Andy B. Anderson; John Michael Oakes, and Michael Fraser. 1994. "Environmental Equity: The Demographics of Dumping." *Demography* 31(2): 229–48.

Arendt, Hannah. 1973. *The Origins of Totalitarianism.* New York: Harcourt Brace Jovanovich.

Aronoff, Marilyn, and Valerie Gunter. 1992. "Defining Disaster: Local Constructions for Recovery in the Aftermath of Chemical Contamination." *Social Problems* 39(4): 345–65.

Aronskind, Ricardo. 2001. *¿Más Cerca o Más Lejos del Desarrollo? Transformaciones Económicas en los '90.* Buenos Aires: Centro Rojas.

Ashforth, Adam. 2005. *Witchcraft, Violence, and Democracy in South Africa.* Chicago: University of Chicago Press.

Auyero, Javier. 1999. " 'This Is Like the Bronx, Isn't It?' Lived Experiences of Slum-dwellers in Argentina." *International Journal of Urban and Regional Research* 23(1): 45–69.

———. 2001. *Poor People's Politics.* Durham, NC: Duke University Press.

———. 2002. *La Protesta.* Buenos Aires: Centro Cultural Rojas, Serie Extramuros.

———. 2007. *Routine Politics and Collective Violence in Argentina: The Gray Zone of State Power.* Cambridge: Cambridge University Press.

Beamish, Thomas. 2000. "Accumulating Trouble: Complex Organization, a Culture of Silence, and a Secret Spill." *Social Problems* 47(4): 473–98.

———. 2001. "Environmental Hazard and Institutional Betrayal." *Organization and Environment* 14(1): 5–33.

Becker, Howard. 1958. "Problems of Inference and Proof in Participant Observation." *American Sociological Review* 23(6): 652–60.

———. 1995. "Visual Sociology, Documentary Photography, and Photojournalism: It's (Almost) All a Matter of Context." *Visual Sociology* 10(1–2): 5–14.

Berney, Barbara. 2000. "Round and Round It Goes. The Epidemiology of Childhood Lead Poisoning, 1950–1990." In *Illness and the Environment: A Reader in Contested Medicine,* ed. Steve Kroll-Smith, Phil Brown, and Valerie J. Gunter, 235–57. New York: New York University Press.

Bourdieu, Pierre. 1977. *Outline of a Theory of Practice*. Cambridge: Cambridge University Press.

——. 1991. *Language and Symbolic Power*. Cambridge: Harvard University Press.

——. 1998. *Practical Reason*. Stanford, CA: Stanford University Press.

——. 2000. *Pascalian Meditations*. Stanford, CA: Stanford University Press.

Bourdieu, Pierre, Jean-Claude Chamboderon, and Jean-Claude Passeron. 1991. *The Craft of Sociology: Epistemological Preliminaries*. New York: Aldine De Gruyter.

Bourdieu, Pierre, and Marie-Claire Bourdieu. 2004. "The Peasant and Photography." *Ethnography* 5(4): 601–16.

Bourdieu, Pierre, and Loïc Wacquant. 1992. *An Invitation to Reflexive Sociology*. Chicago: University of Chicago Press.

Bourdieu, Pierre, et al. 1999. *The Weight of the World: Social Suffering in Contemporary Society*. Stanford, CA: Stanford University Press.

Bourgois, Philippe. 2001. "The Power of Violence in War and Peace." *Ethnography* 2(1): 5–34.

——. 2003 [1995]. *In Search of Respect: Selling Crack in El Barrio*. Second edition with new postface. Cambridge: Cambridge University Press.

Bourgois, Philippe, and Jeffrey Schonberg. Forthcoming. *Righteous Dopefiend*. Berkeley: University of California Press.

Brown, Phil. 1991. "The Popular Epidemiology Approach to Toxic Waste Contamination." In *Communities at Risk: Collective Responses to Technological Hazards*, ed. Stephen Robert Couch and J. Stephen Kroll-Smith, 133–55. New York: Peter Lang.

Brown, Phil, and Judith Kirwan Kelley. 2000. "Physicians' Knowledge, Attitudes, and Practice Regarding Environmental Health Hazards." In *Illness and the Environment: A Reader in Contested Medicine*, ed. Steve Kroll-Smith, Phil Brown, and Valerie J. Gunter, 46–71. New York: New York University Press.

Brown, Phil, Steve Kroll-Smith, and Valerie J. Gunter. 2000. "Knowledge, Citizens, and Organizations. An Overview of Environments, Diseases, and Social Conflict." In *Illness and the Environment: A Reader in Contested Medicine*, ed. Steve Kroll-Smith, Phil Brown, and Valerie J. Gunter, 9–25. New York: New York University Press.

Brown, Phil, and Edwin Mikkelsen. 1990. *No Safe Place: Toxic Waste, Leukemia, and Community Action*. Berkeley: University of California Press.

Bryson, Lois, Kathleen McPhillips, and Kathryn Robinson. 2001. "Turning Public Issues into Private Troubles. Lead Contamination, Domestic Labor, and the Exploitation of Women's Unpaid Labor in Australia." *Gender and Society* 15(5): 754–72.

Bullard, Robert. 1990. *Dumping in Dixie: Race, Class, and Environmental Quality*. Boulder, CO: Westview Press.

——, ed. 1993. *Confronting Environmental Racism: Voices from the Grassroots*. Boston, MA: South End Press.

——, ed. 2005. *The Quest for Environmental Justice*. San Francisco: Sierra Club Books.

Burawoy, Michael, et al. 2000. *Global Ethnography*. Berkeley: University of California Press.

Cable, Sherry, and Edward Walsh. 1991. "The Emergence of Environmental Protest: Yellow Creek and TMI Compared." In *Communities at Risk: Collective Responses to Technological Hazards*, ed. Stephen Robert Couch and J. Stephen Kroll-Smith, 113–32. New York: Peter Lang.

Capek, Stella. 1993. "The 'Environmental Justice' Frame: A Conceptual Discussion and Application." *Social Problems* 41(1): 5–24.

Caplan, Pat. 2000. "Introduction: Risk Revisited." In *Risk Revisited*, ed. Pat Caplan, 1–28. London: Pluto Press.

Castells, Manuel. 2002. "Preface. Sustainable Cities: Structure and Agency." In *Livable Cities? Urban Struggles for Livelihood and Sustainability*, ed. Peter Evans, ix–xi. Berkeley: University of California Press.

Catenazzi, Andrea and Juan D. Lombardo. 2003. *La Cuestión Urban en los Noventa en la Región Metropolitana de Buenos Aires*. Buenos Aires: Universidad Nacional de General Sarmiento, Instituto del Conurbano.

Cerulo, Karen. 2006. *Never Saw It Coming: Cultural Challenges to Envisioning the Worst*. Chicago: University of Chicago Press.

Checker, Melissa. 2005. *Polluted Promises: Environmental Racism and the Search for Justice in a Southern Town*. New York: New York University Press.

Clapp, Richard. 2002. "Popular Epidemiology in Three Contaminated Communities." *Annals of the American Academy of Political and Social Science* 584 (November): 35–46.

Clarke, Lee. 1989. *Acceptable Risk? Making Decisions in a Toxic Environment*. Berkeley: University of California Press.

Clarke, Lee, and James F. Short. 1993. "Social Organization and Risk: Some Current Controversies." *Annual Review of Sociology* 19:375–99.

Cole, L., and S. Foster. 2001. *From the Ground Up: Environmental Racism and the Rise of the Environmental Justice Movement*. New York: New York University Press.

Couch, Stephen Robert, and J. Stephen Kroll-Smith, eds. 1991. *Communities at Risk: Collective Responses to Technological Hazards*. New York: Peter Lang.

Cravino, María Cristina. 2006. *Las Villas de la Ciudad: Mercado e Informalidad Urbana*. Los Polvorines: Universidad de General Sarmiento.

———. 2007a. "Política Habitacional para Asentamientos Informales en el Área Metropolitana de Buenos Aires. Nuevos Escenarios y Viejos Paradigma Aggiornados." Unpublished manuscript. Los Polvorines: Universidad de General Sarmiento.

———. 2007b. "Transformaciones Urbanas y Mercado Inmobiliario Informal en Asentamientos Consolidados del Área Metropolitana de Buenos Aires." Unpublished manuscript. Los Polvorines: Universidad de General Sarmiento.

Croudace, Ian, and Andrew Cundy. 1995. "Heavy Metal and Hydrocarbon Pollution in Recent Sediments from Southampton Water, Southern England: A Geochemical and Isotopic Study." *Environmental Science & Technology* 29(5): 1288–96.

Das, Veena. 1995. *Critical Events: An Anthropological Perspective in Contemporary India*. New York: Oxford University Press.

Das, Veena. 1997. "Sufferings, Theodicies, Disciplinary Practices, Appropriations." *International Social Science Journal* 49(154): 563–72.

Davidson, Pamela, and Douglas Anderton. 2000. "Demographics of Dumping II: A National Environmental Equity Survey and the Distribution of Hazardous Materials Handlers." *Demography* 37(4): 461–66.

Davis, Devra. 2002. *When Smoke Ran Like Water: Tales of Environmental Deception and the Battle against Pollution*. New York: Basic Books.

Davis, Mike. 2006. *Planet of Slums*. London: Verso.

Defensoría del Pueblo de la Ciudad de Buenos Aires. 2006. "Resolución 1157/06." www.defensoria.org.ar.

Defensoría del Pueblo de la Nación Argentina. 2003. *Informe Especial sobre la Cuenca Matanza-Riachuelo*. Defensor del Pueblo de la Nación, Argentina.

De Jesus, Carolina. 2003. *Child of the Dark: The Diary of Carolina Maria de Jesus*. New York: Signet.

DelVecchio Good, Mary-Jo, Paul E. Brodwin, Byron Good, and Arthur Kleinman. 1991. *Pain as Human Experience: An Anthropological Perspective*. Berkeley: University of California Press.

DiMaggio, Paul. 1997. "Culture and Cognition." *Annual Review of Sociology* 23: 263–87.

Dorado, Carlos. 2006. "Informe sobre Dock Sud." Unpublished manuscript, Buenos Aires.

Douglas, Mary. 1985. *Risk Acceptability according to the Social Sciences*. New York: Russell Sage Foundation.

Douglas, Mary, and Aaron Wildavksy. 1982. *Risk and Culture*. Berkeley: University of California Press.

Downey, Liam. 2005. "The Unintended Significance of Race: Environmental Racial Inequality in Detroit." *Social Forces* 83(3): 971–1008.

Duneier, Mitchell. 1999. *Sidewalk*. New York: Farrar, Straus, and Giroux.

DuPuis, Melanie, ed. 2004. *Smoke and Mirrors: The Politics and Culture of Air Pollution*. New York: New York University Press.

Durkheim, Emile, and Marcel Mauss. 1963. *Primitive Classification*. Chicago: University of Chicago Press.

Eagleton, Terry. 1991. *Ideology: An Introduction*. London: Verso.

Eckstein, Susan. 1990. "Urbanization Revisited: Inner-city Slum of Hope and Squatter Settlement of Despair." *World Development* 18(2): 165–81.

Edelstein, Michael. 2003. *Contaminated Communities*. Boulder, CO: Westview Press.

Eden, Lynn. 2004. *Whole World on Fire: Organizations, Knowledge and Nuclear Weapons Devastation*. Ithaca, NY: Cornell University Press.

Elias, Norbert. 2004. *Compromiso y Distanciamiento*. España: Península.

Emirbayer, Mustafa, and Ann Mische. 1998. "What Is Agency?" *American Journal of Sociology* 103(4): 962–1023.

Engels, F. [1844] 1973. *The Condition of the Working Class in England.* London: Lawrence and Wishart.

Erikson, Kai. 1976. *Everything in Its Path: Destruction of Community in the Buffalo Creek Flood.* New York: Simon & Schuster.

Evans, Gary W., and Elyse Kantrowitz. 2002. "Socioeconomic Status and Health: The Potential Role of Environmental Risk Exposure." *Annual Review of Public Health* 23: 303–31.

Evans, Peter, ed. 2002. *Livable Cities? Urban Struggles for Livelihood and Sustainability.* Berkeley: University of California Press.

Farmer, Paul. 2003. *Pathologies of Power: Health, Human Rigths, and the New War on the Poor.* Berkeley: University of California Press.

———. 2004. "An Anthropology of Structural Violence." *Current Anthropology* 45(3): 305–25.

Flaherty, Michael. 1999. *A Watched Pot: How We Experience Time.* New York: New York University Press.

Freudenburg, William. 1993. "Risk and Recreancy: Weber, the Division of Labor, and the Rationality of Risk Perceptions." *Social Forces* 71(4): 909–32.

Freund, Peter E. S. 1988. "Bringing Society into the Body: Understanding Socialized Human Nature." *Theory and Society* 17(6): 839–64.

Gaventa, John. 1980. *Power and Powerlessness: Quiescence and Rebellion in an Appalachian Valley.* Urbana: University of Illinois Press.

Geertz, Clifford. 1973. *The Interpretation of Cultures.* New York: Basic Books.

Giddens, Anthony. 1986. *The Constitution of Society.* New York: Polity Press.

Gilovich, Thomas, Dale Griffin, and Daniel Kahneman, eds. 2002. *Heuristics and Biases: The Psychology of Intuitive Judgment.* Cambridge: Cambridge University Press.

Goldstein, Donna. 2003. *Laughter Out of Place: Race, Class, Violence, and Sexuality in a Rio Shantytown.* Berkeley: University of California Press.

González de la Rocha, Mercedes, et al. 2004. "From the Marginality of the 1960s to the 'New Poverty' of Today: A LARR Research Forum." *Latin American Research Review* 39(1): 184–203.

Gould, Kenneth A. 1998. "Response to Eric J. Krieg's 'The Two Faces of Toxic Waste: Trends in the Spread of Environmental Hazards.'" *Sociological Forum* 13(1): 21–23.

Greenpeace. 2001. "Zona de Riesgo." www.greenpeace.org.ar.

Grillo, Oscar, Monica Lacarrieu, and Liliana Raggio. 1995. *Políticas Sociales y Estrategias Habitacionales.* Buenos Aires: Espacio Editorial.

Harper, Douglas. 1997. "Visualizing Structure: Reading Surfaces of Social Life." *Qualitative Sociology* 20(1): 57–77.

———. 2002. "Talking about Pictures: A Case for Photo Elicitation," *Visual Studies* 17(1): 13–26.

———. 2003. "Framing Photographic Ethnography: A Case Study." *Ethnography* 4(2): 241–66.

Hayward, Mark, and Bridget Gorman. 2004. "The Long Arm of Childhood: The Influence of Early-life Social Conditions on Men's Mortality." *Demography* 41(1): 87–107.

Heimer, Carol. 1988. "Social Structure, Psychology, and the Estimation of Risk." *Annual Review of Sociology* 14: 491–519.

———. 2001. "Cases and Biographies: An Essay on Routinization and the Nature of Comparison." *Annual Review of Sociology* 27: 47–76.

Hirschfeld, Lawrence. 1994. "The Child's Representation of Human Groups." *The Psychology of Learning and Motivation*. 31: 133–85.

Hochstetler, Kathryn, and Margaret Keck. 2007. *The Greening of Brazil: Environmental Activism in State and Society*. Durham, NC: Duke University Press.

Hoffman, Kelly, and Miguel Angel Centeno. 2003. "The Lopsided Continent: Inequality in Latin America." *Annual Review of Sociology* 29: 363–90.

Huntley, S. L., N. L. Bonnevie, and R. J. Wenning. 1995. "Polycyclic Aromatic Hydrocarbon and Petroleum Hydrocarbon Contamination in Sediment from the Newark Bay Estuary, New Jersey." *Archives of Environmental Contamination and Toxicology* 28(1): 93–107.

Iturbe, Rosario, Rosa Flores, Carlos Flores, and Luis Torres. 2006. "Cleanup Levels at an Oil Distribution and Storage Station in Eastern Central Mexico Determined from a Health Risk Assessment." *International Journal of Environment and Pollution* 26(1–3): 106–128.

Jasanoff, Sheila. 1986. *Risk Management and Political Culture*. New York: Russell Sage Foundation.

Kahneman, Daniel, Paul Slovic, and Amos Tversky. 1982. *Judgment under Uncertainty: Heuristics and Biases*. New York: Cambridge University Press.

Katz, Jack. 1982. "A Theory of Qualitative Methodology: The Social System of Analytic Fieldwork." In Jack Katz, *Poor People's Lawyers in Transition*. New Brunswick, NJ: Rutgers University Press.

———. 1999. *How Emotions Work*. Chicago: Chicago University Press.

———. 2001. "From How to Why. On Luminous Description and Causal Inference in Ethnography (Part I)." *Ethnography* 2(4): 443–73.

———. 2002. "From How to Why. On Luminous Description and Causal Inference in Ethnography (Part II)." *Ethnography* 3(1): 73–90.

Kleinman, Arthur. 1988. *The Illness Narratives: Suffering, Healing, and the Human Condition*. New York: Basic Books.

Kleinman, Arthur, Veena Das, and Margaret Lock, eds. 1997. *Social Suffering*. Berkeley: University of California Press.

Klinenberg, Eric. 2002. *Heat Wave: A Social Autopsy of Disaster in Chicago*. Chicago: University of Chicago Press.

Krieg, Eric J. 1998. "The Two Faces of Toxic Waste: Trends in the Spread of Environmental Hazards." *Sociological Forum* 13(1): 3–20.

Kroll-Smith, Steve, Phil Brown, and Valerie J. Gunter, eds. 2001. *Illness and the Environment: A Reader in Contested Medicine.* New York: New York University Press.

Kroll-Smith, Stephen, and Stephen Robert Couch. 1991. "Technological Hazards, Adaptation and Social Change." In *Communities at Risk: Collective Responses to Technological Hazards,* ed. Stephen Robert Couch and J. Stephen Kroll-Smith, 293–320. New York: Peter Lang.

Lanzetta, Máximo, and Néstor Spósito. 2004. "Proceso Apell Dock Sud." Unpublished manuscript.

Last, Murray. 1992. "The Importance of Knowing about Not Knowing: Observations from Hausaland." In *The Social Basis of Health and Healing in Africa,* ed. Steven Feierman and John M. Janzen, 393–406. Berkeley: University of California Press.

Leder, Drew. 1984. "Medicine and Paradigms of Embodiment." *Journal of Medicine and Philosophy* 9: 29–43.

———. 1990. *The Absent Body.* Chicago: Chicago University Press.

Lemos, Maria Carmen de Mello. 1998. "The Politics of Pollution Control in Brazil: State Actors and Social Movements Cleaning Up Cubatao." *World Development* 26(1): 75–87.

Lerner, Steve. 2005. *Diamond: A Struggle for Environmental Justice in Louisiana's Chemical Corridor.* Cambridge, MA: MIT Press.

Levinas, Emmanuel. 1988. "Useless Suffering." In *The Provocation of Levinas: Rethinking the Other,* ed. R. Bernasconi and D. Wood, 156–67. London: Routledge.

Levine, Adeline Gordon. 1982. *Love Canal: Science, Politics, and People.* Toronto: Lexington Books.

Lock, Margaret. 1993. "Cultivating the Body: Anthropology and Epistemologies of Bodily Practice and Knowledge." *Annual Review of Anthropology* 22: 33–55.

Lomnitz, Larissa. 1975. *Cómo sobreviven los marginados.* Mexico: Siglo XXI.

MacGill, Sally. 1989. "Risk Perceptions and the Public: Insights from Research around Sellafield." In *Environmental Threats: Perception, Analysis and Management,* ed. J. Brown, 48–66. London: Belhaven Press.

Mansbridge, Jane, and Aldon Morris, eds. 2001. *Oppositional Consciousness: The Subjective Roots of Protest.* Chicago: Chicago University Press.

Marcantonio, F., G. C. Flowers, and N. Templin. 2000. "Lead Contamination in a Wetland Watershed: Isotopes as Fingerprints of Pollution." *Environmental Geology* 39(9): 1070–76.

Markowitz, Gerald, and David Rosner. 2002. *Deceit and Denial: The Deadly Politics of Industrial Pollution.* Berkeley: University of California Press.

Massey, Doreen. 1994. *Space, Place, and Gender.* Minneapolis: University of Minnesota Press.

Mazur, Allan. 1991. "Putting Radon and Love Canal on the Public Agenda" In *Communities at Risk: Collective Responses to Technological Hazards,* ed. Stephen Robert Couch and J. Stephen Kroll-Smith, 183–203. New York: Peter Lang.

McAdam, Doug. 1982. *Political Process and the Development of Black Insurgency 1930–1970.* Chicago: Chicago University Press.

Merlinsky, Gabriela. 2007a. Conflicto Ambiental, Organizaciones y Territorio en el Area Metropolitana de Buenos Aires. Unpublished manuscript. Universidad de General Sarmiento, Buenos Aires.

——. 2007b. "Vulnerabilidad Social y Riesgo Ambiental: ¿Un Plano Invisible para las Políticas Públicas?" *Mundo Urbano* 27. www.mundourbano.unq.edu.

Miller, Dale T. and Debora A. Prentice. 1994. "Collective Errors and Errors about the Collective." *Personality and Social Psychology Bulletin.* 20: 541–50.

Mintz, Sidney. 2000. "Sows' Ears and Silver Linings: A Backward Look at Ethnography." *Current Anthropology* 41(2): 169–89.

Mitchell, Jerry, Déborah Thomas, and Susan Cutter. 1999. "Dumping in Dixie Revisited: The Evolution of Environmental Injustices in South Carolina." *Social Science Quarterly* 80(2): 229–43.

Morris, David. 1997. "About Suffering: Voice, Genre, and Moral Community." In *Social Suffering,* ed. Arthur Kleinman, Veena Das, and Margaret Lock, 25–45. Berkeley: University of California Press.

Murphree, David, Stuart Wright, and Helen Rose Ebaugh. 1996. "Toxic Waste Siting and Community Resistance: How Cooptation of Local Citizen Opposition Failed." *Sociological Perspectives* 39(4): 447–63.

Murray, Melbin. 1978. "The Colonization of Time," in *Timing Space and Spacing Time in Social Organization,* ed. T. Carlstein et al. London: Edward Arnold.

Myhen, Gabe. 2004. *Ulrick Beck: A Critical Introduction to the Risk Society.* London, UK: Pluto Press.

Narayan, Kirin. 1993. "How Native Is a 'Native' Anthropologist?" *American Anthropologist* 95(3): 671–686.

Neuwirth, Robert. 2005. *Shadow Cities: A Billion Squatters, A New Urban World.* New York: Routledge.

Nguyen Vinh-Kim, and Karine Peschard. 2003. "Anthropology, Inequality, and Disease: A Review." *Annual Review of Anthropology* 32: 447–74.

Ohnuki-Tierney, Emiko. 1984. " 'Native' Anthropologists." *American Ethnologist* 11(3): 584–86.

Ortner, Sherry. 1995. "Resistance and the Problem of Ethnographic Refusal." *Comparative Studies in Society and History* 37(1): 173–93.

——. 2006. *Anthropology and Social Theory.* Durham, NC: Duke University Press.

PAE *Plan de Acción Estratégico para la Gestión Ambiental Sustentable de un Area Urbano-industrial a Escala Completa.* 2003. *Informe Final.* JMB Ingeniería Ambiental.

Paley, Julia. 2001. *Marketing Democracy: Power and Social Movements in Post-dictatorship Chile.* Berkeley: University of California Press.

Pellow, David. 2002. *Garbage Wars: The Struggle for Environmental Justice in Chicago.* Cambridge, MA: MIT Press.

———. 2005. "Environmental Racism: Inequality in a Toxic World." In *The Blackwell Companion to Social Inequalities*, ed. Mary Romero and Eric Margolis, 147–64. Malden, MA: Blackwell.

Perrow, Charles. 1984. *Normal Accidents*. New York: Basic Books.

———. 1997. "Organizing for Environmental Destruction." *Organization and Environment* 10: 66–72.

———. 1999. *Normal Accidents*. New York: Basic Books.

Petryna, Adriana. 2002. *Life Exposed: Biological Citizens after Chernobyl*. Princeton, NJ: Princeton University Press.

Pezzoli, Keith. 2000. *Human Settlements and Planning for Ecological Sustainability: The Case of Mexico City*. Cambridge, MA: MIT Press.

Phillimore, Peter, Suzanne Moffatt, Eve Hudson, and Dawn Downey. 2000. "Pollution, Politics, and Uncertainty. Environmental Epidemiology in North-east England." In *Illness and the Environment: A Reader in Contested Medicine*, ed. Steve Kroll-Smith, Phil Brown, and Valerie J. Gunter, 217–34. New York: New York University Press.

Pirez, Pedro. 2001. "Buenos Aires: Fragmentation and Privatization of the Metropolitan City." *Environment and Urbanization* 14(1): 145–58.

Polletta, Francesca. 2006. *It Was Like a Fever: Storytelling in Protest and Politics*. Chicago: University of Chicago Press.

Portés, Alejandro. 1972. "Rationality in the Slum: An Essay in Interpretive Sociology." *Comparative Studies in Society and History* 14(3): 268–86.

Proctor, Robert. 1995. *Cancer Wars: How Politics Shapes What We Know and Don't Know about Cancer*. New York: Basic Books.

Rao, Vyjayanthi. 2006. "Slum as Theory: The South/Asian City and Globalization." *International Journal of Urban and Regional Research* 30(1): 225–32.

Reilly, J. 1999. "Just Another Food Scare? Public Understanding of the BSE Crisis." In *The Nation's Diet: The Social Science of Food Choice*, ed. G. Philo, 44–59. London: Longman.

Rock, David. 1987. *Argentina, 1516–1982: From Spanish Colonization to Alfonsin*. Berkeley: University of California Press.

Roth, Julius. 1963. *Timetables: Structuring the Passage of Time in Hospital Treatment and Other Careers*. Indianapolis: Bobbs-Merrill.

Sayad, Abdelmalek. 2004. *The Suffering of the Immigrant*. Malden, MA: Polity Press.

Scarry, Elaine. 1987. *The Body in Pain: The Making and Unmaking of the World*. New York: Oxford University Press.

Scheper-Hughes, Nancy. 1992. *Death without Weeping*. Berkeley: University of California Press.

———. 2005. "Death Squads and Democracy in Northeast Brazil." In *2005 Report of the Harry Frank Guggenheim Foundation*, 43–56.

Scheper-Hughes, Nancy, and Margaret Lock. 1987. "The Mindful Body: A Prolegomenon to Future Work in Medical Anthropology." *Medical Anthropology Quarterly* 1(1): 6–41.

Schutz, Alfred. 1964. *The Problem of Social Reality: Collected Papers 1.* The Hague: Martinus Nijhoff.

Scott, James, and Benedict Kerkvliet. 1977. "How Traditional Rural Patrons Lose Legitimacy: A Theory with Special Reference to Southeast Asia." In *Friends, Followers, and Factions: A Reader in Political Clientelism,* ed. Laura Guasti, Carl Landé, Steffen Schmidt, and James Scott, 439–58. Berkeley: University of California Press.

Silvestri, Graciela. 2004. *El color del rio: Historia cultural del paisaje del riachuelo.* Buenos Aires: Universidad Nacional de Quilmes.

Skinner, Jonathan. 2000. "The Eruption of Chances Peak, Monserrat, and the Narrative Containment of Risk." In *Risk Revisited,* ed. Pat Caplan, 156–83. London: Pluto Press.

Snow, David. E., and Robert Benford. 1988. "Ideology, Frame Resonance, and Participant Mobilizaton." In *From Structure to Action: Comparing Social Movement Research,* ed. B. Klandermans, H. Kriesi, and S. Tarrow, 197–217. Greenwich, CT: JAI Press.

Sorokin, Pitirim, and Robert Merton. 1937. "Social Time: A Methodological and Functional Analysis." *American Journal of Sociology* 42: 615–29.

Stallings, Robert A. 1990. "Media Discourse and the Social Construction of Risk." *Social Problems* 37: 80–95.

Steinberg, Mark. 1999. *Fighting Words: Working-class Formation, Collective Action, and Discourse in Early Nineteenth-century England.* Ithaca, NY: Cornell University Press.

Stillwaggon, Eileen. 1998. *Stunted Lives, Stagnant Economies: Poverty, Disease, and Underdevelopment.* New Brunswick, NJ: Rutgers University Press.

Svampa, Maristella. 2001. *Los que ganaron: La vida en los countries y barrios privados.* Buenos Aires: Biblos.

Tarrow, Sidney. 1998. *Power in Movement.* Cambridge: Cambridge University Press.

Thomas, V. M. 1995. "The Elimination of Lead in Gasoline." *Annual Review of Energy and the Environment* 20: 301–324.

Thompson, John B. 1984. *Studies in the Theory of Ideology.* Berkeley: University of California Press.

Tierney, Kathleen. 1999. "Toward a Critical Sociology of Risk." *Sociological Forum* 14(2): 215–42.

Tilly, Charles. 1978. *From Mobilization to Revolution.* New York: McGraw-Hill.

——. 1986. *The Contentious French.* Cambridge, MA: Harvard University Press.

——. 1996. "Invisible Elbow." *Sociological Forum* 11(4): 589–601.

——. 1998. *Durable Inequality.* Berkeley: University of California Press.

——. 2006. *Regimes and Repertoires.* Chicago: University of Chicago Press.

Todeschini, Maya. 2001. "The Bomb's Womb? Women and the Atom Bomb." In *Remaking a World: Violence, Suffering and Recovery,* ed. Veena Das, Arthur Kleinman, Margaret Lock, Mamphela Ramphele, and Pamela Reynolds, 102–56. Berkeley: University of California Press.

Torrado, Susana. 2004. *La Herencia del Ajuste.* Buenos Aires: Capital Intelectual.

United Nations Human Settlements Programme. 2003. *The Challenge of Slums: Global Report on Human Settlements 2003*. London: Earthscan Publications.

Van Parijs, Philippe, ed. 1993. *Arguing for Basic Income: Ethical Foundations for a Radical Reform*. London: Verso.

Van Wolputte, 2004. "Hang on to Your Self: Of Bodies, Embodiment, and Selves." *Annual Review of Anthropology* 33: 251–69.

Vaughan, Diane. 1990. "Autonomy, Interdependence, and Social Control: NASA and the Space Shuttle Challenger." *Administrative Science Quarterly* 35(2): 225–57.

——. 1998. "Rational Choice, Situated Action, and the Social Control of Organizations." *Law and Society Review* 32(1): 23–61.

——. 1999. "The Dark Side of Organizations: Mistake, Misconduct, and Disaster." *Annual Review of Sociology* 25: 271–305.

——. 2004. "Theorizing Disaster: Analogy, Historical Ethnography, and the Challenger Accident." *Ethnography* 5(3): 315–47.

Wacquant, Loïc. 1995. "The Pugilistic Point of View: How Boxers Think and Feel about Their Trade." *Theory and Society* 24: 489–535.

——. 2002. "Scrutinizing the Street: Poverty, Morality, and the Pitfall of Urban Ethnography." *American Journal of Sociology* 107(6): 1468–1532.

——. 2003. "Ethnographeast: A Progress Report on the Practice and Promise of Ethnography." *Ethnography* 4: 5–14.

——. 2004a. *Body and Soul: Notebooks of an Apprentice Boxer*. New York: Oxford University Press.

——. 2004b. "Comment on Farmer." *Current Anthropology* 45(3): 322.

——. 2004c. "Following Pierre Bourdieu into the Field." *Ethnography* 5(4): 387–414.

——. 2005. "Carnal Connections: On Embodiment, Apprenticeship, and Membership." *Qualitative Sociology* 28(4): 445–74.

——. 2007. *Urban Outcasts: A Comparative Sociology of Advanced Marginality*. New York: Polity Press.

Wagner, Jon. 2001. "Does Image-based Field Work Have More to Gain from Extending or from Rejecting Scientific Realism?" *Visual Sociology* 16(2): 7–21.

Walsh, Edward. 1981. "Resource Mobilization and Citizen Protest in Communities around Three Mile Island." *Social Problems* 29 (1): 1–21.

Walsh, Edward, Rex Warland, and D. Clayton Smith. 1993. "Backyards, NIMBYs, and Incinerator Sitings: Implications for Social Movement Theory." *Social Problems* 41(1): 25–38.

Warren, Christian. 2000. *Brush with Death: A Social History of Lead Poisoning*. Baltimore: Johns Hopkins University Press.

Weinberg, Adam S. 1998. "The Environmental Justice Debate: A Commentary on Methodological Issues and Practical Concerns." *Sociological Forum* 13(1): 25–32.

Weyland, Kurt. 2005. "Theories of Policy Diffusion: Lessons from Latin American Pension Reform." *World Politics* 57: 262–95.

Widener, Patricia. 2000. "Lead Contamination in the 1990s and Beyond. A Follow-up." In *Illness and the Environment: A Reader in Contested Medicine*, ed. Steve Kroll-Smith, Phil Brown, and Valerie J. Gunter, 260–69. New York: New York University Press.

Wilkinson, Iain. 2005. *Suffering: A Sociological Introduction*. Cambridge, UK: Polity Press.

Williams, Raymond. 1977. *Marxism and Literature*. New York: Oxford University Press.

Willis, Paul. 1977. *Learning to Labor*. New York: Columbia University Press.

Willis, Paul, and Mats Trondman. 2000. "Manifesto for Ethnography." *Ethnography* 1(1): 5–16.

Wolford, Wendy. 2006. "The Difference Ethnography Can Make: Understanding Social Mobilization and Development in the Brazilian Northeast." *Qualitative Sociology* 29(3): 335–52.

Wright, Angus. 2005. *The Death of Ramón González: The Modern Agricultural Dilemma*. Austin: University of Texas Press.

Yujnovsky, Oscar. 1984. *Las claves políticas del problema habitacional argentino*. Buenos Aires: Grupo Editor Latinoamericano.

Zerubavel, Eviatar. 1979. *Patterns of Time in Hospital Life*. Chicago: University of Chicago Press.

Zonabend, Françoise. 1993. *The Nuclear Peninsula*. New York: Cambridge University Press.

# Index